Seafood

Omega-3s For Healthy Living

by Evie Hansen

Thanks to:

Pete Berg, cover design
Alaska Seafood Marketing Institute, cover photo
Fusion Studios, graphic design and production
Al Tietjen, illustrations
Carol McDougall, editing
Liz Edward, recipe research and testing
Ryna Hansen, RN, health research

Contact the publisher for reproduction or ordering requests at:
National Seafood Educators, P.O. Box 60006
Richmond Beach, Washington 98160
206.546.6410
information@SeafoodEducators.com

Library of Congress Cataloging-in-Publication data has been applied for.
ISBN 978-0-9616426-6-2
Includes bibliographical references and index

Printed in the United States of America

First Edition

10 9 8 7 6 5 4 3 2 **1**   Digit in bold indicates the number of this printing.

Seafood

Omega-3s For Healthy Living

To my wonderful husband and
beautiful daughter who took me up on
my offer when I said "If you catch it,
I'll cook it."

Randy and Mickey, Kodiak, Alaksa

Other books by the author:

Seafood Treasures
Seafood-A Collection of Heart Healthy Recipes
Seafood-A Collection of Heart Healthy Recipes, Second Edition
Selling Seafood
Light-Hearted Seafood
Seafood-Twice A Week
Seafood Grilling -Twice A Week

What others are saying:

"There is a nutrition revolution going on, and Evie Hansen is in the forefront of the action."
Dallas Morning News

"If you like fish but want to know more, this book's for you."
The Miami Herald

"The tops in healthful reading and recipes."
U.S.A Today

"The recipes are quick and nutritious, besides being flavorful and appealing."
Bon Appetit

"...a dieters dream."
Cosmopolitan

Contents

Chapter 3

How To Introduce, Buy, & Cook Seafood

Chapter 4
All About Seafood

Chapter 5
Appetizers

Chapter 6
Soups

Chapter 7
Salads

Chapter 8
Sandwiches

Chapter 9
Pasta, Noodles and Rice

Introduction

My fascination with seafood began at an early age. Dad was a commercial fisherman trolling off the Pacific coast bringing home salmon, rockfish and anything that swam for our meals: digging razor clams, racking Willapa oysters, and trout fishing were natural parts of my childhood entertainment. Along with seafood harvesting came cleaning, preparing, smoking, pickling, canning, freezing and cooking it. With all I did, I found that I had fun, too.

There were snickers around the dorm when a college friend teased, "You can serve smoked salmon rather than cake at your wedding reception." We did!

My husband, Randy, taught fisheries at the University of Washington for several years. That was where I became fascinated with the research on omega-3 fatty acids. Dr. Maurice Stansby, Dr. Kenneth Chew and Dr. George Pigott, internationally recognized seafood authorities, graciously opened their offices to my ever-probing nutrition questions.

Worldwide seafood and health research studies were just emerging and fish and shellfish were receiving rave reviews. The research was unbiased and coming from reputable, peer-reviewed scientists and doctors.

In 1977, I founded National Seafood Educators. It is a lofty name for a fisherman's daughter and wife, but I knew this exciting seafood research needed to reach the American consumer, and it was sitting in dusty, archived boxes.

In 1982, National Seafood Educators organized the nation's first seafood and health campaign cosponsored by the American Heart Association. This dusted off the research boxes and the consumer response was overwhelming! I've lived out of my suitcase ever since, crossing the country, teaching, cooking and inspiring you.

Enjoy *Seafood Omega-3s For Healthy Living.* Make it yours—add more chilies, use fresh herbs, make your own twist—whatever helps you and your family eat more fish and shellfish.

How To Use This Book

To help you eat more seafood, the recipes in this book were chosen for ease of preparation, convenient ingredients, life changing healthy results and great taste.

Remember, it's not a single species of seafood but the entire meal you eat, day after day, year after year, that builds a lifetime of health benefits. Eating a diverse diet of fish and shellfish along with fruits, vegetables and whole grains that meet dietary guidelines can improve health and longevity. The recommendations in this book are for the general public, not anyone under 2 years of age.

This book is not intended to serve as a replacement for the advice of a physician. Take it to your doctor or nutritionist and ask him or her to review it. A health care professional should be consulted prior to including more seafood in your diet.

How were the recipes calculated?

First Data Base Nutritionist Pro was used. The first ingredient listed was calculated.

Alternatives and garnishes were not included in calculations.

Why were certain ingredients chosen?

Nutrient content, taste, texture, color, availability, cost and variety were deciding factors for choosing ingredients. You can make ingredient substitutions depending on your supplies, time and budget.

For instance:

• Fresh and frozen seafood were used interchangeably.

• Virgin olive and canola oil were used in recipe testing.

• Dried herbs and spices were used instead of fresh for convenience and availability. When fresh were used, it is specified. To convert recipes to fresh herbs, multiply the suggested amount 3 times.

• Refined table salt was used but sea salt adds exceptional flavor and texture, especially when used in a salad or as a finishing salt.

Equivalent Measures:
    oz. = ounce
    lb. = pound
    C.   = cup
    T.   = tablespoon
    tsp. = teaspoon
    Pinch or Dash = 1/16 teaspoon

A serving of seafood is 3 ounces cooked.

Chapter 1

All About Omega-3s

Omega-3s Are Essential

The message is simple.
Our bodily functions require omega-3s.
Our bodies can't make omega-3s.
Our diet must provide omega-3s.

> *"Knowing is not enough, we must apply.*
> *Willing is not enough, we must do."*
> **---Goethe 1749-1832.**

What's So Healthy About Omega-3s?

Researchers were astounded over 30 years ago when they discovered several large populations that had significantly low, almost nonexistent, levels of heart disease. This included the native Inuit peoples of Greenland who have long consumed large amounts of seafood that are naturally high in omega-3 fatty acids; the Japanese, who eat 10 times more seafood than today's Americans; Scandinavians, Dutch, Sardinians, and those Americans who regularly eat seafood.

Scientific research in recent years established the vital health benefits of regularly eating omega-3s from seafood. Dr. Dariush Mozaffarian, Harvard School of Public Health, says, "Seafood is likely the single most important food one can consume for good health." The healthfulness is attributed to unique oils found in fish and shellfish called omega-3 fatty acids. The 2006 Institute of Medicine, *Seafood Choices*, an extensive and independent review, emphasizes the benefits of eating seafood.

Omega-3s Vital Role For The Body

Omega-3s ensure that our cells make energy in the body for daily activities and enhance functions such as blood pressure and blood clotting. In addition, they protect our cells, block out harmful substances that try to get in, and assist in the production of beneficial body chemicals that fight off invaders that cause inflammation in the bloodstream, joints, and tissues.

The Body Needs Healthy Fat

Fat is used in the body to form cells, and is especially crucial in growth and development. There are various types of fat, consisting of chemical chains of fatty acids. Not all fat, however, is the same.

What Are the Different Types of Omega-3s?

It is important to be on a first name basis with the omega-3 fatty acid family. Each family member has a different responsibility in keeping the body healthy. The most important omega-3 family members are EPA and DHA found abundantly and almost solely in seafood. ALA is a lesser part of the omega-3 family.

> *Did you know?*
> *Because of the importance of* EPA *and* DHA, *they were awarded a rare heart-health nutrient claim by the* Food *and* Drug Administation (FDA). ALA *was not.*

- EPA (eicosapentaenoic acid) is a powerhouse omega-3. Its primary value is its strong anti-inflammatory effect, immune enhancement and cardiovascular health.
- DHA (docosahexaenoic acid) is a powerhouse for brain function, visual acuity and signal transmissions.
- ALA (alpha-linolenic acid) is the omega-3 family member found in vegetable sources such as algae, flaxseed, kale and nuts as well as in seafood. ALA, however, is not as beneficial as EPA/DHA omega-3s from seafood sources.

Content of Omega-3s

(EPA-20:5) and (DHA-22:6)
3 ounces, cooked

	EPA mg.	DHA mg.
Blue Crab	210	200
Catfish	40	100
Cod	80	150
Flounder/Sole	210	220
Haddock	60	140
Halibut	70	320
Lobster	40	30
Ocean Perch	80	230
Orange Roughy	20	NA
Oyster	750	430
Pollock	80	390
Rockfish	155	220
Trout, Rainbow	400	440
Salmon		
sockeye, atlantic, coho	280	950
chum, pink	450	740
Scallop	70	80
Shrimp	145	120
Swordfish	120	600
Tilapia	60	130
Tuna	200	540

How Many Omega-3s Are Enough?

The United States Institute of Medicine set an intake level of 1600mg of all omega-3s per day for men and 1100 mg for women. One 3-ounce serving of salmon contains 1825mg of omega-3s (ALA/EPA/DHA). A panel of experts convened by the American Association for the Advancement of Science has confirmed the health benefits of omega-3s and has made a recommendation to eat 4-7 servings of seafood a week. The new food pyramid put out by the United States Department of Agriculture (USDA) suggests choosing fatty fish more often for lunch and dinner.

Can You Have Too Many Omega-3s?

It is generally agreed that a person can't overdose by eating one daily serving of a variety of fish and shellfish. If you are on medications, ask your healthcare provider about the potential interactions of omega-3s with your prescription drugs.

How Long Will It Take To Improve Overall Health?

Gary Small M.D., professor of Psychiatry and Biobehavioral Sciences at the UCLA School of Medicine studied two groups of people. His findings, presented at the American College of Neuropsychopharmacology's annual meeting, showed that older participants who combined a healthy regime including omega-3s, physical and mental exercises, and stress reduction, demonstrated measurable memory and brain improvements.

Fernando Holguim, M.D. of the Emory University School of Medicine in Atlanta found it took two weeks to increase heart rate variability – a marker for a healthy heart.

Should I Take Omega-3 Pills?

Seafood contains vitamins A, C, D, and E, selenium, protein, iron, potassium, and over 40 hard-to-find trace minerals that are essential to the human body. A fish oil pill may not contain all of these essential nutrients. The American Dietetic Association states, "There is something about whole food that when it goes into the body it's more than 90% absorbed, while [with] a supplement you absorb only about 50%." Eating more seafood aids in lowering your overall intake of total and saturated fat and encourages you to combine it with other nutritious foods, such as fruits, vegetables and whole grains.

When you eat seafood, you receive a forkful of nutritional benefits.

How Do Omega-3s Get In My Eggs, Cheeses, Muffins?

Chickens, sheep, cattle, goats and deer freely foraged on grasses, twigs and bugs before manufactured agriculture. As a result, their eggs, cheeses, milk and meat naturally produced omega-3s (ALA). Today, however, massive farms feed animals an atypical diet. If farmers purchase feed fortified with fish oils containing EPA & DHA, or flax seeds (ALA), their animals will produce eggs, cheeses and meats containing some omega-3s (ALA, EPA, DHA). Muffins, breads, crackers, and other foods may be baked with fish oils and or flax seed resulting in omega-3s appearing on the product label.

Some countries have laws protecting the nutrient content and name of a food. For instance, the Italian government has specific requirements for labeling cheese Pecorino Romano. This guarantees omega-3s in their cheese by assuring the animals feed and lifestyle is the same as centuries ago. Pecorino Romano cheese today is just like it was centuries ago. The same is true for wild seafood.

Food manufacturers are cashing in on omega-3s as an ingredient. There will be hundreds of products fortified with omega-3s on the market including ice cream, hummus, and milk. It will be necessary to analyze costs and read nutrition labels and to be aware of increased calories, sodium, fat and sugar.

> **Did you know?**
> Current labeling laws do not require the manufacturer to designate which omega-3 family member is in their fortified food.

Americans Need An Oil Change

Most Americans need more omega-3s, instead of omega-6s. Omega-6s are commonly found in refined vegetable oils including safflower, corn, sunflower, cotton seed, and soybean oils. These oils are in many processed foods such as cereals, bread, and chips. During food processing, omega-6s are also chemically manipulated to become harmful hydrogenated oils and trans fats. These oils are commonly found in margarines, muffins, shelf-stable snacks, cookies, crackers, French fries, donuts, and other fried foods. Read nutrition labels carefully!

What you need to know about Omega-6 foods

Ongoing research shows that the standard American diet contains too many omega-6 foods and not enough foods high in omega-3s. In healthy diets found around the world, such as the Mediterranean Diet, people thrive on a balanced ratio of 1:1 omega-3s to omega-6s. This diet includes a generous amount of fish, whole grains, fresh fruits, vegetables, and olive oil. Americans, however, eat so much highly processed and refined foods that the ratio in many diets is as great as 20:1, or more!

Joseph R. Hibbeln, M.D. of the National Institute of Health (NIH) says, "due to increased use of vegetable oils in processed foods in the last 100 years, there has been a 1,000 fold increase in [the consumption of] omega-6 fatty acids." Dr. Artemis P. Simopoulos, President of The Center for Genetics, Nutrition, and Health in Washington, D.C. reports, "This imbalance can be a risk factor for many health problems, including cardiovascular disease, arthritis, obesity, and diabetes. It has also been implicated in brain disorders from depression to schizophrenia and even Alzheimer's."

Omega-3 Benefits

Heart Health

There is a tremendous amount of worldwide research indicating that EPA and DHA omega-3s may reduce the risk of cardiovascular disease. Omega-3s from seafood may help our hearts in the following ways:
- maintain normal heart rhythms
- reduce inflammation
- reduce the chance of stroke
- lubricate red blood cells so they become more slippery and slide through closing arteries reducing the possible formation of blood clots
- relax the walls of blood vessels.

Brain Nourishment

When I was growing up, fish was considered brain food. I was told that eating fish was good for us and would make us smart. There is evidence now that this old food lore may have some scientific basis. Studies show that DHA is absolutely critical during fetal and infant brain development, and it remains essential to cognitive function throughout life. Omega-3s feed the brain to regulate mood, attention and memory.

Omega-3s researcher Andrew L. Stoll, M.D., Director of the Psychopharmacology Research Laboratory at Harvard's McLean Hospital relates, "Emerging studies show that omega-3 fatty acids may have therapeutic value in the treatment of:

– depression

– postpartum depression

– stress

– schizophrenia

– Attention Deficit Hyperactivity Disorder

– Manic/Depressive (Bipolar Disorder)."

In geographic areas where there is a high consumption of DHA omega-3s there is a decreased rate of depression, according to an abstract published in Psychiatric Clinics of North America.

Do omega-3s increase intelligence? The first long-term study on prenatal omega-3 fatty acids intake suggests they may make children smarter. Ingrid Helland, M.D., of the University of Oslo in Norway, studied 431 pregnant women who were given cod liver oil with about 2.5 grams of omega-3s. Four years later, 84 children whose mothers had taken cod liver oil tested significantly higher on mental processing, as compared with children whose mothers had taken corn oil - omega-6s.

A United Kingdom study of 9,000 mothers and children suggested those mothers who consumed less of the essential omega-3s had children with lower IQs.

Start eating seafood today! Women in childbearing years can't begin soon enough.

Did you know?

The only survivor of the West Virginia Sago Mine disaster suffered from brain damage. His neurosurgeon turned to omega-3s. Backed by sound scientific research, Julian Bailes, M.D., gave miner Randal McCloy EPA & DHA. Today, Bailes credits the nutrients with playing a big role in McCloy's recovery by helping decrease brain inflammation and repairing the brain.

Alzheimer's Disease

Alzheimer's is, in part, an inflammatory disease. Dutch researchers examined the eating habits of 900 elderly men. They found that the men who ate more fish high in omega-3s had the best mental function and the men whose diets were highest in omega-6 fatty acids were more likely to suffer from dementia.

Did you know?
A seven year study reported in the Archives of Neurology concluded that "Participants who consumed fish once per week or more had 60% less risk of Alzheimer's disease compared with those who rarely or never ate fish."

Healthy Mothers, Healthy Babies, Healthy Children

A pregnant woman needs extra omega-3s because the rapidly growing brain of her fetus uses omega-3s from her body. This crucial fat, necessary 3-4 weeks after conception, is used by the fetus for building brain tissue, for nerve growth and for the development of the eyes' retinas. A mother who eats plenty of fish will give her baby generous amounts of omega-3s by nourishing the fetus through her body and later by breastfeeding. Regular seafood consumption during pregnancy may also prolong gestation, reducing incidence of premature birth and increasing average birth weight. At a recent Seafood and Health Alliance conference held in Washington, D.C., scientists revealed that premature infants have less omega-3s in their tissues than full-term infants. Pregnant and nursing women, as a result, need to be encouraged to eat more seafood.

Did you know?
After birth, the brain continues to grow for the next two years. For that reason, seafood with DHA

omega-3s are important in early life. Breastfeeding ensures that infants obtain omega-3s from mother's milk.

Eye Health

Frequently eating fish high in omega-3s will nourish and protect the eyes, according to the American Journal of Clinical Nutrition (AJCN). The AJCN reports on its diet study of over 70,000 men and women, the omega-3s in fish may protect against age-related macular degeneration. Once macular degeneration sets in, increasing EPA/DHA omega-3s may retard the process. According to another study published in the American Journal of Epidemiology, women whose diets were higher in omega-3s had a lower risk of developing cataracts and macular degeneration.

Two recent studies published in the Archives of Ophthalmology report that consumption of omega-3s improves eye health. A study on 681 elderly men, led by Dr. Johanna Seddon of the Massachusetts Eye and Ear Infirmary in Boston, found that those who ate fish twice a week had a 36% lower risk of age-related macular degeneration. A separate study of 2,335 Australian men and women over a five-year period found that those who ate fish once a week reduced their risk of macular degeneration by 40%.

A 2005 report showed that women who eat fish containing omega-3s decreased their risk of developing Dry Eye Syndrome (DES), often a problem with aging when the body produces less oil.

Diabetes

If type 2 diabetes were an infectious disease, passed from one person to another, public health officials would say we're in the midst of an epidemic. The good news is that type 2 diabetes is largely preventable. Diet and nutrition are linked to the prevention and treatment of diabetes and its complications. Tune-up your diet with more seafood.

Studies suggest that overweight people who follow a weight loss program including exercise, tend to achieve better control over their blood sugar and cholesterol levels when fish rich in omega-3s is a staple in their low fat diet.

The type of fats in your diet can also affect the development of diabetes. Good fats, such as the polyunsaturated fats found in fish and shellfish may help ward off type 2 diabetes. Eating fatty fish may protect you against a heart attack if you already have diabetes.

Did you know?
The American Diabetes Association nutritional guidelines for people who already have diabetes recommends eating at least two servings of non-fried fish per week.

Cancer
Results are promising on the continuing research of the beneficial role of omega-3s in cancer. Potential benefits of eating low saturated fat seafood include:
– helping healthy cells resist damage from tumor-producing cells
– interfering with tumor growth
– inhibiting the spread of the tumor throughout the body.

Ongoing studies of prostate, colon, and breast cancer promise emerging information for many years.

Did you know?
The most recent research will be published on www.seafoodeducators.com.

Weight Loss
Eating more protein from seafood can help increase levels of a hunger-fighting hormone called peptide YY. British scientist, Rachael Batterham, of University College, London reports, "We've now found that increasing the protein content of the diet augments the body's peptide YY helping to reduce hunger and aid weight loss."

Eating fish rich in omega-3 fatty acids (such as salmon, mackerel, and herring) is a staple in a low-fat diet, according to the University of Maryland Medical Center.

The Australian Satiety Index ranks steamed white fish such as halibut and cod as the number-one most filling food out of 38 common foods. A study in Sweden found that people ate 11 percent less at dinner after having fish for lunch versus those who ate a beef lunch.

The same is true for children, who, according to reports, are getting heavier and at a younger age. Samuel S. Gidding, M.D., Professor of Pediatric Cardiology at Jefferson Medical College in Philadelphia, states, "If children consume too many calories of extra fat or sugar, they may consume excess calories leading to weight gain. This may cause them to not meet their nutritional requirements, leading to numerous physical and mental health problems."

Follow these weight loss tips:

• Stock up on frozen fish and shellfish. Today's "frozen at sea" or "flash frozen" technology means that premium quality frozen seafood is readily available.

• Cook frozen seafood directly from the freezer.

• Select water-packed tuna over oil-packed varieties, as it is significantly lower in calories. For example, a 3½ -ounce can of drained, oil packed tuna contains 200 calories while drained, water-packed tuna has only 131 calories.

• Store several cans or pouches of salmon, tuna, sardines or mackerel in the refrigerator, so they'll be chilled and ready to make a quick and easy sandwich or salad.

• Surimi products (imitation seafood) are an inexpensive and low calorie addition to a diet plan. Surimi products, made from very lean white fish such as pollock, are only 99 calories per $3^1/_2$-ounce serving.

• Serve a seafood appetizer or soup before dinner to curb your appetite; broiled shrimp spritzed with lemon/lime juice or smoked salmon with a tray of fresh-cut vegetables.

• Save time by cooking two seafood meals at the same time, serving one immediately and refrigerating the second for lunch tomorrow.

• Seafood grilling is a dieter's dream.

Skin

Feed your face? Literally! What you eat can affect wrinkling, sun damage, bruising and thin skin according to Dr. Nicholas V. Perricone M.D., Assistant Clinical Professor of Dermatology at Yale Medical School. Eating a diet of yellow or orange fruits, dark green leafy vegetables, whole grains, nuts, olive oil and fatty fish may preserve tissue elasticity, slow down aging and protect against sun. Research is on-going with a variety of skin disorders such as psoriasis and acne.

Longer Life

A long healthy life is no accident. It begins with good genes, and it also depends on good habits. Scientists at U.S. National Institute on Aging focused on several regions where people live significantly longer; Sardinia, Okinawa, and Loma Linda, California produce a high number of centurions. These elderly suffer a fraction of the diseases that commonly kill people in other parts of the world, and enjoy more active and healthy years of life. These populations are aware of the need for eating omega-3s and their diet includes them. On the Sardinian's table are grass fed dairy products. The Okinawan people eat vegetables, miso soup, tofu and fish daily. The Seventh Day Adventists from Loma Linda, California who eat whole grains, fruits, vegetables and nuts tend to live 4 to 10 years longer than the average Californian.

Having a balanced life of exercising, eating a variety of unprocessed foods (try at least one new healthful food each week), not smoking, and practicing moderation in all areas will improve your health and longevity.

Even if you haven't been eating many omega-3s, start today. Enjoy this adventure with seafood!

Chapter 2

More Nutritional Benefits of Eating Seafood

Seafood is one of the most healthful foods you can eat! Check out these nutritional rewards.

Low in Calories

Most fish and shellfish contain less than 100 calories per 3-oz. cooked serving. Compare that with 160 calories for a similar portion of chicken and more than 200 calories for beef! Steaming, grilling or poaching seafood will result in a delicious meal without added oil.

Did you know?
The calorie count of seafood is so low because it is about 60% water.

Low in Cholesterol

For many years it was believed that all shellfish were high in cholesterol. Improved technology has shown that this is not the case. Studies show that eating shellfish does not increase cholesterol or triglyceride levels. Cholesterol belongs to a family of compounds known as sterols. Included in the sterol family, however, are a number of non-cholesterol sterols. Early values did not distinguish cholesterol from these non-cholesterol sterols. We now understand that non-cholesterol sterols found in shellfish interfere with the absorption of cholesterol, allowing it to pass right through the body.

To understand the shellfish/cholesterol picture, it is important to know that there are two kinds of shellfish: mollusks and crustaceans.

Mollusks have less cholesterol, ounce for ounce, than any other protein source. Clams, mussels, and oysters are mollusks known as "vegetarians of the sea" because they eat tiny sea plants. Shrimp, crab and lobster are crustaceans that feed on small sea animals in addition to plants. Because they eat more cholesterol, they contain slightly more cholesterol.

> **Did you know?**
> Most shellfish contains less than 115 milligrams of cholesterol and low levels of saturated fat.

3-oz. Cooked Product	Cholesterol (milligrams)	Saturated Fat (grams)
lobster, steamed	72	0.1
chicken breast, baked	85	1.0
pork chop, baked	86	9.3
blue crab, steamed	100	0.2
shrimp, steamed	166	0.2
ground beef, 10% fat, broiled	72	4.0

Good Source of Calcium

National data shows that most American children over age 8 don't get enough calcium, a deficiency that increases their risks for developing osteoporosis in adulthood. Evidence suggests that bone fractures may be on the rise in adolescents and adults, possibly because of a lack of calcium combined with a decrease in exercise, which helps with bone-strengthening. Drinking a glass of milk is not the only way to get your calcium.

Seafood is an additional source of calcium. Eighty-four percent of America's most popular fish and shellfish contain calcium; the best sources are crab, oysters, clams, shrimp, ocean perch, herring, and rainbow trout. Canned anchovies, jack mackerel, salmon and sardines provide high levels of calcium if processed with bones, which are soft and easy to eat. In addition, the oils in seafood contain vitamin D, the key vitamin to aid in absorbing the calcium into your body.

High-Quality Protein

The excellent quality protein in seafood is complete, meaning it contains all eight essential amino acids. A 3-oz. serving provides about half the protein the body needs each day and is low in fat and cholesterol. Because seafood has a unique connective tissue structure, it is easy to chew and digest, perfect for children, the elderly, and those with red meat intolerance. Ounce for ounce, it contains considerably more omega-3s than skinless chicken, for a similar number of calories.

Low In Sodium

Salt and fresh water fish are naturally low in sodium. When cooking, add herbs and spices to enhance taste. Some commercially cooked crab meat may be high in sodium. Purchase live crab or lobster and cook it with celery, onions and other non salt seasoning, dramatically reducing the amount of sodium. Most crustaceans and mollusks are somewhat higher in sodium than fish, but relatively low compared with other foods. If your doctor has told you to watch your salt intake, seafood is a healthful low-sodium choice.

> **Did you know?**
> To lower the sodium in canned products, rinse the seafood for one minute under cold running water in a colander. It will reduce the sodium by 40%.

Zero Carbohydrates

Most fish have zero carbohydrates, although crustaceans and mollusks have a small amount. Breading and deep-frying seafood adds carbohydrates and may add harmful trans-fats.

Low Glycemic Index

The glycemic index (G.I.) measures the amount of carbohydrates each food contains on a scale of 0 to 100, according to how much blood sugar is raised after eating. Since most fish don't have any carbohydrates, there is no glycemic index for fish. Shellfish such as mussels, crab, squid, and oysters have a very low G.I. To find the glycemic index of your favorite foods, go to http://www.glycemicindex.com. This is a handy search feature to instantly observe a food's G.I. rating. Remember, lower is better.

Good Source of Vitamins and Minerals

Seafood boasts over 40 essential vitamins and minerals, according to Dr. Heber, a University of Washington Professor Emeritus. Mussels, for instance, are a good source of Vitamin C, and oysters provide iron. Seafood is the richest source of chromium, selenium, iodine, vanadium, zinc and copper, elements necessary for blood sugar metabolism and weight management. The zinc found in clams and oysters supports reproductive health and regulates digestive juices. Crab, clams, oysters, shrimp, ocean perch and rainbow trout contain more calcium, potassium and magnesium than many other protein sources. Canned anchovies, jack mackerel, salmon

NUTRITION FACTS
3 oz./84 g cooked edible portion*

Food	Calories	Calories from Fat	Total Fat (g)	Total Fat (%DV)	Saturated Fat (g)	Saturated Fat (%DV)	Cholesterol (mg)	Cholesterol (%DV)	Sodium (mg)	Sodium (%DV)	Total Carbohydrates (g)	Total Carbohydrates (%DV)	Protein (g)	Vitamin A (%DV)	Vitamin C (%DV)	Calcium (%DV)	Iron (%DV)
Blue Crab	100	10	1	2	0	0	95	32	330	14	0	0	20	0	4	10	4
Catfish	130	60	6	9	2	10	50	17	40	2	0	0	17	0	0	0	0
Clams 12 Small	110	15	1.5	2	0	0	80	27	95	4	6	2	17	10	0	8	30
Cod	90	5	1	1	0	0	50	17	65	3	0	0	20	20	2	2	2
Flounder/Sole	100	15	1.5	2	0	0	55	18	100	4	0	0	19	0	0	2	0
Haddock	100	10	1	2	0	0	70	23	85	4	0	0	21	2	0	2	6
Halibut	120	15	2	3	0	0	40	13	60	3	0	0	23	4	0	2	6
Lobster	80	0	0.5	1	0	0	60	20	320	13	1	0	17	2	0	6	2
Ocean Perch	110	20	2	3	0.5	3	45	15	95	4	0	0	21	0	2	10	4
Orange Roughy	80	5	1	2	0	0	20	7	70	3	0	0	16	2	0	4	2
Oysters 12 Medium	100	35	4	6	1	5	80	27	300	13	6	2	10	0	6	6	45
Pollock	100	10	1	2	0	0	80	27	110	5	0	0	20	2	0	0	2
Rainbow Trout	140	50	6	9	2	10	55	18	35	1	0	0	20	4	4	8	2
Rockfish	100	15	2	3	0	0	40	13	70	3	0	0	21	4	0	2	2
Salmon Atlantic/Coho/Sockeye	190	90	10	15	2	10	70	23	55	2	0	0	24	4	4	2	2
Salmon Chum/Pink	130	40	4	6	1	5	70	23	65	3	0	0	22	2	0	2	4
Scallops 6 Large/12 Medium	140	10	1	2	0	0	65	22	310	13	5	2	27	0	0	4	14
Shrimp	100	10	1.5	2	0	0	170	57	240	10	0	0	21	4	0	6	10
Swordfish	120	50	6	9	1.5	8	40	13	100	4	0	0	16	2	4	0	4
Tilapia	110	20	2.5	4	1	5	75	25	30	1	0	0	22	4	2	0	2
Tuna	130	15	1.5	2	0	0	50	17	40	2	0	0	26	2	2	2	4

*Based on a 2,000 calorie diet   Data from FDA Federal Register/ Vol. 71, No. 159, August 17, 2006 - Appendix D to Part 101 "Nutrition Facts for Cooked Fish"

See also page 33

NUTRITION FACTS
3 oz./84 g cooked edible portion*

Food	Calories	Calories from Fat (g)	Total Fat g	Total Fat %DV	Saturated Fat g	Saturated Fat %DV	Cholesterol mg	Cholesterol %DV	Sodium mg	Sodium %DV	Total Carbohydrates g	Total Carbohydrates %DV	Protein g	Protein %DV	Vitamin A %DV	Vitamin C %DV	Calcium %DV	Iron %DV
Crab, Dungeness	90	11	1	2	0	0	65	22	320	13	1	0	19	2	2	6	6	2
Crab, Imitation (Surimi)	90	9	1	2	0	0	20	7	720	30	9	3	10	2	2	0	2	2
Crab, Snow	100	10	1	2	0	0	60	20	590	25	0	0	20	4	4	10	4	14
Crayfish	70	5	1	2	0	0	115	38	80	3	0	0	15	0	0	0	4	6
Grouper	100	18	2	2	0.5	3	40	13	45	2	0	0	21	4	4	0	2	6
Herring	210	63	15	23	3.5	18	85	28	80	3	0	0	18	2	2	0	10	6
Mackerel	170	51	9	14	2.5	13	50	17	95	4	0	0	22	4	0	2	2	8
Mahi-Mahi	90	38	1	2	N/A	N/A	80	27	95	4	0	0	20	4	4	0	2	6
Monkfish	80	18	2	3	0.5	3	30	10	20	1	6	2	16	0	0	2	0	2
Mussels	150	23	4	6	0.5	3	50	17	315	13	6	2	20	6	6	20	2	32
Octopus	140	13	2	3	0.5	3	80	27	390	16	4	1	25	6	6	10	10	45
Sea Bass	110	28	2	3	0.5	3	45	15	75	3	0	0	20	4	4	0	2	2
Snapper	100	18	1.5	2	0	0	40	13	70	3	0	0	21	4	4	6	4	6
Squid	150	4	6	9	1.5	8	220	73	260	11	7	2	15	0	0	0	4	6
Turbot	100	13	3	5	N/A	N/A	50	17	160	7	0	0	17	0	0	6	2	2
Whitefish	150	27	6	9	1	5	65	22	55	2	0	0	21	2	2	2	4	2
Whiting	100	9	1.5	2	0.5	3	70	23	110	5	0	0	20	2	2	0	6	2

Data from USDA Table 16-1, 2004

and sardines provide high levels of calcium if processed with bones.

Vitamin D, which aids in absorbing calcium and which many Americans are deficient in, is found in fatty fish. In the body, it is transformed into a benevolent hormone, shoring up our bones, regulating cell growth and helping prevent the kind of wild cell proliferation that leads to cancer. Dr. Michael F. Holick, a vitamin D researcher at Boston University, is finding promising connections and improvements in heart disease, multiple sclerosis, diabetes, rheumatoid arthritis and gum disease.

Food Sources for Vitamin D		Internal Units
cod liver oil	1 tablespoon	1360 IU
salmon, cooked	$3^1/_2$ ounces	360 IU
mackerel, cooked	$3^1/_2$ ounces	345 IU
tuna, canned in oil	3 ounces	200 IU
sardines, canned in oil	$1^1/_2$ ounces	250 IU
milk, all types, fortified	1 cup	98 IU

Add These Healthful Foods to Your Seafood Meals

Nearly 2,500 years ago, Hippocrates is credited with saying, "Let food be thy medicine and medicine be thy food." Science has proved that Hippocrates was on to something—namely, that the food we eat may prevent and, in some cases, fight disease. Add beneficial foods to your seafood meals and you will be on your way to better health and living longer.

Fruits and Vegetables

The Japanese find it so important to eat food in a variety of colors that they educate the population to eat a minimum of 15 different foods each day for optimum health. Eating a colorful variety of fruits and vegetables provides a wide, rich range of vitamins and minerals, and an excellent source of fiber and phytochemicals (naturally occurring plant chemicals) your body uses to stay healthy and energetic. One serving (1/2 C. or size of tennis ball) of fruits and vegetables may contain 100 different phytochemicals, thought to maintain a healthy weight, protect against the effects of aging, help lower blood pressure and reduce the risk of cancer and heart diseases. Fruits and vegetables are low in calories, most are fat-free and a good source of water (over 50%). Eat a mix of raw and cooked vegetables to gain maximum benefits from phytochemicals.

Did you know?
A significant reduction of illnesses is seen when individuals consume 7-10 servings of fruits and vegetables daily. Try to eat all colors every day!

Red Fruits and Vegetables
Specific phytochemicals in the red food group which are being studied for their health-promoting properties include anthocyanins and lycopene, a cancer fighting antioxidant. Some studies suggest that lycopene especially helps to protect against prostate cancer.

Did you know?
More than 85% of the lycopene in the North American diet comes from tomatoes and tomato-based products.

How to Get the Nutrients You Need
- *Top baked cod with chopped basil and sliced tomatoes.*
- *Use tomato-based salsas as a delicious tartar sauce alternative.*
- *Slice red bell peppers into tuna stir-fry or steamed mussels.*
- *Chop pickled beets and red apples into herring salad.*
- *Top grilled salmon with cranberry salsa.*
- *Bake crusty halibut and steam Swiss chard.*
- *Poach red potatoes with sablefish or bluefish.*
- *Serve a dessert fruit platter of raspberries, strawberries or watermelon.*

Yellow/Orange Fruits and Vegetables
Yellow/orange fruits and vegetables contain varying amounts of antioxidants. Antioxidants protect the health

of every cell in the body. Oxygen, essential for life, can create damaging by-products, called free radicals. Antioxidants work to bind free radicals. If left unchecked, free radicals may cause heart damage, cancer, cataracts and a weak immune system.

Examples of antioxidants are beta carotene, vitamins C, E, and selenium.

How to Get the Nutrients You Need
- *Make corn relish and serve with grilled sea bass.*
- *Bake a sweet potato alongside your oven-roasted seafood.*
- *Spritz lemon juice over shrimp or crab salad.*
- *Roast quartered Finnish potatoes beside salmon topped with pineapple slices.*
- *Bake butternut squash or other winter squash with your seafood dinner.*
- *Celebrate! Treat family and friends to a homemade pumpkin or sweet potato pie.*

White/Brown Fruits and Vegetables

White, tan, and brown fruits and vegetables contain varying amounts of phytochemicals that may offer some protection against cancer. These include allicin, found in the garlic and onion family. World-wide studies have suggested garlic may protect against stomach, prostate and colorectal cancers.

How to Get the Nutrients You Need
- *Slice garlic, ginger, sweet onions as a base for stir-fried, steamed or poached seafood.*
- *Mix sliced bananas, shredded coconut and chopped dates into a seafood salad.*
- *Roast parsnips, rutabagas, white potatoes and salmon on a wood baking plank.*
- *Spritz lime juice over jicama slices and cooked shrimp. Serve as an appetizer.*
- *Steam cauliflower alongside salmon steaks.*
- *Add mushrooms to Cioppino or Fishermen's Stew.*

Green Fruits and Vegetables

Green vegetables contain varying amounts of phytochemicals such as lutein and indoles. They have potential antioxidant health-promoting benefits. Change salad greens from iceburg lettuce, which has little nutritional value, to dark, colorful greens such as spinach, arugula, mesclun- even romaine lettuce. The more color, the better!

How to Get the Nutrients You Need
- *Slice avocados over crab salad or add to Fantastic Quesadillas.*
- *Steam asparagus, green beans or broccoli alongside a salmon fillet.*
- *Roast a whole vegetable stuffed salmon for Thanksgiving dinner. Garnish with roasted Brussel sprouts.*
- *Include chilies in salsas, sauces or toppings to kick up nutritional benefits and flavor.*
- *Seed, slice, lightly salt and chill cucumbers in the refrigerator for 30 minutes. Serve with grilled tuna.*
- *Make a salad of sliced grapes, honeydew melon and pears. Top with surimi, flaked coconut and fresh squeezed lime juice.*

Blue/Purple Fruits and Vegetables
Blue/purple fruits and vegetables contain varying amounts of health-promoting phytochemicals such as anthocyanins and phenolics, currently being studied for their potential antioxidant and anti-aging benefits.

How to Get the Nutrients You Need
- *Add purple cabbage to your coleslaw.*
- *Make blueberry salsa and serve with steamed cod.*
- *Add raisins to your shrimp curry.*
- *Garnish crab, shrimp, and crawfish salad with black olives.*
- *Serve a dish of blackberries for dessert.*

Whole Grains
Here's a nutritional bargain for your buck! Nutrient dense unrefined grains such as oats, corn meal, wheat berries, wheat germ, bulgur, wild and brown rice and amaranth contain fiber to lower blood cholesterol. They are also complex carbohydrates, with vitamins and

minerals that support digestion and balance blood sugar. The nutty flavor of whole grains makes them a perfect accompaniment with seafood to gain a feeling of fullness and satiety.

The cooking time of whole grains may take longer than some seafood. Plan cooking times so that your meal will be ready to serve all together. Whole grains are also great for tomorrow's lunch, so preplan leftovers by doubling the amount. Try using whole grains when making seafood sushi, pasta or stew.

Did you know?

Whole grains are the seed of plants and contain all the parts of the grain, i.e. bran, germ, endosperm. When making seafood sandwiches, buying crackers for dips, or serving bread alongside chowders, it is important that you select foods labeled "whole grains." Products advertised with healthy-sounding words like "oat nut", "cracked wheat" or "12 grain," are usually not whole-grains.

Oils

Most of the recipes in this book use heart-healthy olive and canola oils, rich in unsaturated fat and a source of ALA omega-3s. Extra-virgin olive oil, like all unrefined oils, does not tolerate high heat and has a smoke point of 250°F. It should be used mainly for medium-heat cooking or as a dipping sauce. Use pure or light olive oil for cooking at higher heats because its smoke point is about 410°F. Cooking with high heat doesn't change the basic properties of olive oil, but it does cause the oil to lose some of its flavor. Use canola oil for grilling, broiling, stir-frying and sautéing because it tolerates high heat.

Exposure to heat, oxygen, and light all affect the shelf life of different oils. Oils should be stored in cool and dark areas and sealed so that they are not exposed to air.

Herbs and Spices

I have yet to find an herb or spice that isn't delicious with seafood. Many cultures have known the healing powers of spices, such as garlic, turmeric, mint and many others. Seafood meals regularly seasoned with these herbs may help protect against a variety of health issues.

Heating the spices above 200°F for over 20 minutes will destroy much of their nutritional benefits. Before serving, replenish the herbs you cooked with to freshen up the flavor, increase the nutritional value and attractively decorate the dish.

> ### Did you know?
> The American Cancer Society continues to research the cancer-fighting potential of garlic, ginger and turmeric. At least a dozen clinical trials are underway in the U.S., Israel and England that suggest these herbs and spices may protect against or lower the risk of several cancers.

Fiber

Long heralded as part of a healthy diet, fiber appears to significantly reduce the risk of developing various conditions, including heart disease, adult-onset diabetes, constipation and obesity.

Foods from plants, including fruits, vegetables, whole grains and beans, are the best sources of dietary fiber. To protect your body against some forms of cancer, and to reduce the number of calories it takes to feel full, fill your plate at least two-thirds with fruits, vegetables, whole grains and beans in addition to lean seafood.

> ### Did you know?
> The recipes in this book are deliberately "kicked up" with foods that contain dietary fiber. Feel free to add more to any of the dishes.

Power-packed Seafood Meals

Seafood and other super foods may help you eat your way to better health. For a lifetime of healthy eating, incorporate nutrient-rich foods that will give you wellness and disease prevention benefits. Start today by adding more color, crunch and commitment to your health and well-being.

Chapter 3

How To Introduce, Buy, & Cook Seafood

How do I introduce seafood to my family?

Young Children

During the developmental time in a child's life, you are the biggest influence in establishing positive lifelong eating patterns and habits. If you enjoy seafood, fruits and vegetables, they will. Sharing seafood meals with your young children by giving them bites of boneless seafood from your plate will foster a pattern of eating seafood. It is easy to chew and digest because it doesn't have stringy connective tissues like chicken, pork or beef. Every bite of fish and shellfish is power-packed with essential omega-3s, vitamins and minerals.

In toddlers' "I can do it myself" stage, let them feed themselves, giving them boneless and skinless mild-flavored seafood. Finger foods such as salmon nuggets, cooked shrimp, surimi chunks, poached halibut or cod will be a meal hit. Soon your child will progress to sautéed, steamed or grilled catfish, flounder/sole or tilapia.

• Keep shelf-stable canned or pouched products on hand for an instant meal.

• Make a crunchy sandwich by spreading whole grain bread with light mayonnaise or low-fat plain yogurt, top with cucumber slices and cooked seafood.

• For a kid-friendly snack, lay cooked seafood in a

lettuce leaf and roll it up like a taco or burrito.

The fun begins when younger children can enjoy steamed mussels, scallops or clams in the shell. It's entertaining to have them count the empty shells and compare quantities with other diners.

• Turn an empty shell into a serving dish by filling it with cocktail sauce, tartar sauce or salsa for dipping.

• Wash and save empty shells for a future beach party meal using them for spoons, serving plates and cups. Accompany the meal with beach party music.

Food textures and mouth-feel are an important part of accepting any new food for children. Some kids like a crunchy texture, some like a soft mouth feel. Help them enjoy more seafood by choosing a texture you know they like. Chopped nuts or crushed corn flakes will give a healthy crunch when used as a topping for baked fish. Poached and steamed seafood will have a very soft texture.

Older Children
Invite older children and teenagers to help shop, prepare and cook seafood.

• Get them excited about herbs and spices by letting them sniff or taste and decide which ones to season a dish.

• Suggest family favorite sauces such as teriyaki, sweet and sour, or spicy, then add those familiar seasonings to seafood.

• Encourage them by asking for their seafood meal suggestions. Be prepared for the, "I want lobster or shrimp" request. Reserve higher priced items for birthday, graduation or special occasion celebrations.

• Offer suggestions for adding seafood to pizzas, tacos, sandwiches and salads for quick, easy and nutritious meals.

• Provide seafood snacking plates for after school.

Spouses, Relatives, and Friends
Quite often seafood haters have had a bad experience eating fish or shellfish. They bring histories of dreaded Fish Fridays, fish bones stuck in a throat or foul smelling fishy kitchens. All this is avoidable. Have a good fish talk. Find out what their seafood hang-ups are. Take the list to a trusted seafood counter sales associate and ask

for help. Let them suggest a seafood species that will guarantee meal success. Use the recipes in this book for some quick, tasty options that are sure to win them over.
• Attractively arrange seafood appetizer plates to encourage family and friends to be more experimental.
• Seafood soups, stews and chowders introduce a comforting meal for hesitant fish eaters.
• Smaller bites are less intimidating, especially when trying a new food.
• Create a weekly family "slow down and relax" time before dinner.

Isn't Seafood Expensive?

What is the cost of heart disease? Diabetes? Macular Degeneration? Depression? Alzheimer's? Obesity? Seafood is considered a medical miracle. Health benefits of seafood can be gained by regularly eating 3-ounces of cooked fish or shellfish. Seafood is usually sold by the pound. Dividing the price per pound by 4 will give the cost per serving, the price to pay attention to.

Use these Money Saving Tips:
• Watch for supermarket specials. Buy ahead and freeze.
• Investigate the canned food aisles. Try some of the hundreds of shelf-stable items. One of my favorites is lightly-smoked kippers; another is albacore tuna packed in water.
• Buy seafood trim from the seafood store. Trim are bits and pieces remaining from cutting seafood into steaks, fillets, roasts, etc. There's nothing wrong with them, they are just small pieces. Use trim in chowder, lasagna, sandwich patties or stir-fry.
• Consider buying from fishermen directly.
• Buy a whole fish and cut it into roasts, steaks and fillets. Put the savings in your pocket.
• Get to know the seafood harvesting seasons. Seafood becomes abundant at certain times of the year just like fruits and vegetables. When it's abundant, it usually costs less.
• Treat yourself. What better way to indulge your taste buds than to celebrate and buy seafood you would not ordinarily purchase.

Market Cuts and Types of Seafood

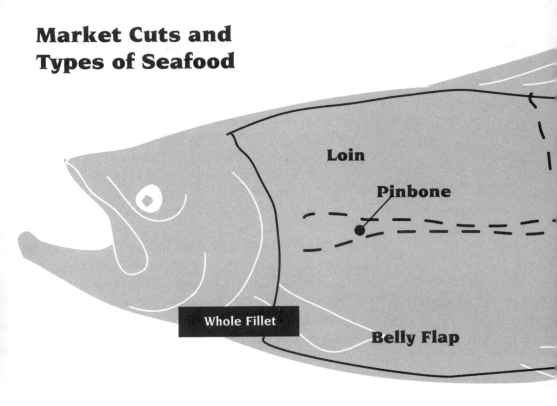

Loin

Pinbone

Whole Fillet

Belly Flap

Buying: At the Market

What cut of seafood should I buy?

Your time, energy, processing skills, equipment and storage space all determine what form of fish and shellfish to buy. There are so many varieties of seafood species, cuts of fish and forms to choose from that you could eat seafood every day, all year long, and not repeat yourself.

Market Cuts of Fish

LIVE: This is straight from the waters, flippin' and kickin'. More stores are offering live seafood; lobster, crab, oysters, catfish, and tilapia are some of the most common choices. People of many cultures have a live seafood tank in their backyard. Transporting and storing live seafood has been documented throughout history. The British Museum has a display of beautiful 16th century porcelain jars that were used to keep fish alive during a long journey.

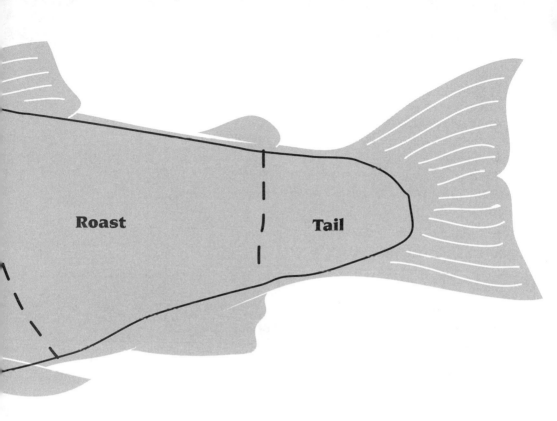

Whole H&G (Headed and Gutted): This is a whole fish with head, scales and guts removed. This form may save money when you cut it into steaks, fillets, roasts or other portions your family will use.

FILLET: Most consumers think fillet means boneless. Not so. If it is boneless, it will be labeled and usually cost more. If it doesn't say boneless on the label, sign or package, it isn't. The same goes for skin on or off. A thin, delicate fillet is a little trickier to cook because it isn't uniform in thickness. Tuck the thin tail under to make for more uniform cooking.

STEAK: The skin is on and the back bone is in a cross-sectional slice, usually ½-inch thick. That makes them great for grilling or broiling. Steaks are easy to turn and more economical than a fillet. Select steaks that are the same thickness for uniform cooking time. It's easy to remove the skin and bones after steaks are cooked and serve them boneless.

Market Types of Shellfish

LIVE: Straight from the water or dug from the sand. Shellfish can live a much longer time out of water than fish can. Properly held oysters are known to stay alive for two weeks.

WHOLE: Shell on, cleaned; fresh or frozen.

SHUCKED, PEELED, SHELLED: Meat only. Shell removed from shellfish.

DEVEINED: Sand intestines removed from shrimp, lobster and other crustaceans.

How do I substitute fish and shellfish?

Does your family hate soft-textured seafood? Do you love to grill fish but don't know which ones to use? The eating characteristics of seafood depend on many things: oil content, harvest location, species, time of year, farmed or wild. The natural texture of seafood can range from soft to firm and meat-like.

Take the **Seafood Substitution Chart** (page 47) to the seafood counter. It will help to compare familiar seafood and give you confidence to substitute unfamiliar species.

What should I look for in live, fresh or freshly thawed seafood?

Fish:

• In general, the flesh should be firm and elastic. When pressed with fingers, it should spring back without leaving a permanent indentation.

• Whole fresh fish should have bright, clear eyes, shiny scales that cling to its skin and bright pink or red gills.

• Fillets should have a firm texture with minimal flaking or separating.

• Steaks and fillets should be moist and free of drying or yellowing around the edges.

Shellfish:

• Live lobster and crabs should move when touched. Lobsters will curl their tails under when handled.

• Live oysters, clams and mussels should "clam up" and close tightly when tapped.

Seafood Substitution Chart

Take this chart with you to the seafood counter. It will help you substitute familiar seafood with what's in season or on sale.

TEXTURE	FLAVOR		
	Mild Very mild, bland	Moderate Balance of mellow and full flavor	Full Rich, bold, assertive
FIRM wild Big, meat- like flakes	Chilean sea bass Monkfish Tilefish Squid Tilapia Halibut Lingcod Kingklip Golden tilefish Grouper Hawaiian sea bass	Catfish, farmed Mahi-mahi Perch Swordfish Tuna, albacore Drum Octopus Clams Tuna	Salmon, sockeye, Salmon, king, wild Carp Shark Marlin

MEDIUM
Versatile,
medium flakes
and firmness
	Cod
	Crayfish
	Black sea bass
	Striped bass
	Sardines
	Oysters
	Sheepshead
	Sea trout
	Walleye pike
	Shrimp
	Black grouper
		Catfish, wild
		Tuna, albacore
		  canned
		Salmon, pink
		  wild, canned
		Mullet
		Shad
		Smelt
		Crab, imitation
		Salmon, chum, wild
		Orange roughy
		Snapper
		Sturgeon
			Salmon, sockeye
			  wild, canned
			Sardines, canned
			Mackerel
			Triggerfish
			Salmon, farmed

DELICATE Tender, soft, small flakes	Croaker Haddock Sole (flounder) Lake perch Pollock, Alaska Pomfret Scallops Spot Sculp (porgy)	Whiting (hake) Salmon, pink, wild Arctic char Crabmeat Buffalo fish Rainbow trout Skate	Bluefish Oysters Mussels, blue

• Shrimp should feel firm to the touch, and have close-fitting shells.

How much seafood should I buy per person?

Worldwide seafood nutritional research has standardized the recommended portion of seafood as 3 ounces cooked, edible portion per person. That's not a lot, about the size of a deck of cards. So when you think of the cost of a pound of seafood versus the health and wellness benefits, seafood comes out a clear winner.

Is frozen seafood as good as fresh?

Shrimp is America's favorite seafood. 96% of all shrimp eaten in America is frozen. Freezing technology has improved to provide good frozen seafood. Processing boats freeze fish within hours of harvesting, so there should be no fear of spoiled fish.

Frozen seafood should be tightly wrapped in an undamaged box or bag and free from moisture crystals.

Cooking from frozen is easy and tasty. Buy frozen fish with confidence.

How do I cook it?

Seafood can be cooked by using all culinary techniques. Methods for cooking seafood, however, can be divided into two general categories: moist or dry-heat cooking.

Dry-Heat Cooking: Grill or Barbecue, Broil, Pan Fry, Sauté, Bake, Oven Roast.

Tips for successful dry-heat cooking:

• Pre-heat all cooking appliances such as grill, fry pan or oven. The quicker seafood is cooked, the less moisture is lost.

• Select fish with high or medium fat content when dry-heat cooking. Fattier fish will stay moist and won't dry out as quickly.

• Cover seafood with sliced vegetables or sauce to retain and slow down the moisture loss while cooking.

• Baste or spray grilled or broiled seafood with a marinade, wine or seasoned liquid, to enhance flavor and

FILLETING A ROUND FISH

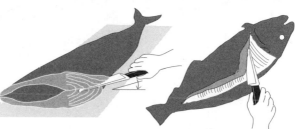

With fish facing away from you, use a sharp, thin-bladed knife. Cut along the back of fish from tail to head. Make a second cut just behind the gills, down to the backbone.

Holding the knife at a slight angle, cut along the bone to free the back side of the fillet.

Peel back the free meat, then cut fillet away from rib cage. Turn fish over and repeat previous steps for second fillet.

FILLETING A FLAT FISH

With the eyed (dark) side of the flat fish up, use a flexible boning knife to make a cut along the spine from the gills to the tail.

Slide the blade between backbone and flesh, lifting fillet away from the bone. Remove the second fillet in the same manner. Turn fish over, repeat.

To skin, grasp fillet by the tail, skin side down. Holding the knife at a slight angle, cut the meat free.

DE-BONING A ROAST

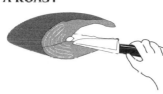

TYING UP A ROAST

With fish lying on its side, slide tip of knife between bone and meat starting at end. Slide knife down length of fish, cutting meat away from bone.

Hold fish on its back, cut from backbone to skin down length of fish, being careful not to cut skin. Repeat for other side. Pull out pinbones with tweezers.

Using heavy meat string, tie fish two or three times around circumference. Tie once or twice around length of roast.

DE-BONING & SKINNING A STEAK

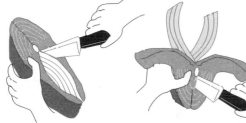

Cut bone away from meat in belly flaps. Repeat on other side.

Turn steak over, cut down from backbone to skin. To butterfly, do not cut through skin flap..

Slide knife under skin at belly flap. Cut meat away by moving knife up along steak until all skin is cut away.

moisture.
- Wrap lean fish in foil or cooking parchment paper to retain more moisture.
- Closely monitor the internal temperature of the fish. When it reaches 145°F., immediately remove it from the heat source.

Grill / Barbecue:
- Pre-heat grill.
- Position grill rack 4 – 6 inches from heat source.
- Place firm textured fillets, at least ½-inches thick, directly on a clean, oiled grill rack. Oil grill surface or coat fish to prevent sticking.
- Marinate lean shrimp and fish to slow down moisture loss.
- Use foil to prevent seafood from falling through the grill. If using wood smoke, poke holes in foil to allow smoke to penetrate the food.
- Use foil to contain marinade or basting sauce. Lay foil on rack, place seafood inside, turn up sides and ends of foil to make a boat. Pour marinade or sauce over seafood.
- Close lid. Use Grill Smokers™, or soaked wood planks to enhance smoky wood flavor.
- Estimate grilling time. Check internal temperature. Immediately remove seafood from grill.

Broil:
- Pre-heat oven broiler. The heat source is very intense and will require close attention.
- Place seafood on a foil-lined oven-proof pan. Keeping the oven door open will remind you to WATCH the seafood.
- Broil, uncovered, 4-5 inches from heat source. Fish fillets under ½-inches thick do not need to be turned over. Thicker pieces of fish will retain more moisture by basting or adding a topping.
- Immediately remove from oven.

Pan Fry / Sauté / Pan Sear:
- Remove moisture from fish and shellfish by patting it dry with paper towels. The drier the raw piece of seafood, the quicker it will brown when cooking.
- Remove the seafood from the refrigerator and let

CLEANING A CLAM

  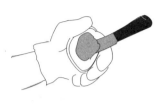

Wash thoroughly, discarding any that have broken shells or that do not close. Wearing a heavy glove, hold the clam in your palm and force the blade of a clam knife between the shells.

Run the knife around the edge of the shell to cut through the muscles holding it together.

Open clam and remove top shell. Use knife to loosen clam from bottom shell. Check for shell fragments before serving.

SHUCKING AN OYSTER

Wash oysters under cold running water and scrub with a stiff brush; discard those that are not tightly closed or that do not close quickly when handled. Place oyster, cupped side down, on a firm surface, holding it with gloved hand. Insert an oyster knife in the side opposite the hinge and twist.

Run the knife around the edge of the shell to cut the muscle that holds the two shells together.

Remove the top shell, and loosen oyster from bottom shell. Check for shell fragments before serving.

CLAMS, OYSTERS, & MUSSELS: To grill, nestle unshucked shellfish in rock salt or crumpled foil. After grilling, top with sauces, salsas, or seasoned butters.

CLEANING A MUSSEL

Prepare mussels as soon as possible after gathering. If mussels must be stored, refrigerate at 35°F. to 40°F. To prepare, scrub shells under cold, running water to remove grass and mud. Discard those that have open shells or shells that do not close quickly with handling.

Clip or pull beard; rinse mussel before cooking.

it sit at room temperature for just a FEW minutes. This will help dry it and bring it up to room temperature. The result will be a beautiful browned piece of seafood and shortened cooking time, which helps the seafood retain more moisture.

- Pre-heat pan to medium high.
- Pour or spray a small amount of oil in pan.
- Add seafood and sauté until golden brown. Estimate total cooking time.
- To keep thicker pieces of fish (½-inches or more) moist, sauté for half the cooking time, turn the fish, then cover the pan with a lid to keep it moist.
- Estimate total cooking time and don't stray too far from the stove.

Bake / Oven Roast:

The next time you are in a restaurant, notice the menu. I think they charge more for items titled "oven-roasted" rather than "baked." It's the same thing.

- Place oven rack in the middle of the oven.
- Pre-heat oven to 450° F.
- Oil the baking dish.
- Pour wine, water or broth in baking dish to retain more moisture.
- Cover or uncover a dish depending on desired outcome. A covered dish will retain more moisture but will not have the golden brown, crusty top. An uncovered dish will dry out quicker, but will bake a beautiful golden brown top.

Tips for Successful Moist-Heat Cooking:

Moist-heat cooking retains more moisture and doesn't dry out the fish or shellfish so fast. It can be a very low calorie cooking method that allows for delicate seafood flavors to show off. Cooking frozen seafood is a fantastic time saver using moist-heat cooking techniques.
To cook rock-hard frozen seafood directly from the freezer, double the cooking time. To enhance the look of moist cooked seafood, finish it under the broiler resulting in a golden brown crust. Enhance the look of moist-cooked seafood by topping it with shredded, chopped, or sliced vegetables, fruits or herbs.

DRESSING A SOFT-SHELL CRAB

 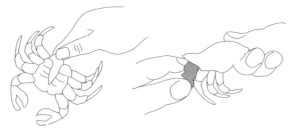 

Remove the apron, the segmented abdominal part beneath the carapace (shell).

Lift the carapace's pointed ends, and remove spongy material.

Using scissors, cut about 1/2 inch behind the eyes and remove the face of the crab. What remains is the edible portion.

DRESSING A HARD-SHELL CRAB

Remove the apron, the segmented abdominal part beneath the carapace (shell).

Hold the back in one hand. Pry off the shell with the other hand.

Pull off and discard the spongy white gills from the body and tiny paddles from the front. Rinse the body well, then drain.

Pull the legs away from the body. Use a pliers or special crab pincers to crack open the leg segments. Remove meat with fingers or special crab pick.

Cut the body in two pieces down the middle (or break apart with hands).

To remove the meat from body, break apart along leg segments, removing meat with fingers or special crab pick.

Steam:

Cooking tools are important. You need a deep pot, steaming rack and lid.

- Add liquid to the pot, add rack. Liquid should not touch seafood.
- Season liquid and seafood with desired herbs, spices, fruits or vegetables.
- Lay seafood on rack, heatproof plate or collapsible vegetable steamer.
- Cover pot with tight lid.
- Turn up heat source until liquid is boiling.
- Reduce heat and steam until done.

Poach:

- Pour an estimated amount of liquid needed to cover seafood in a pan.
- Liquid may be wine, broth, lemon/lime, tomato juice, milk or water.
- Season liquid with vegetables, herbs and spices.
- Simmer poaching liquid for 10 minutes to blend flavors.
- Submerge seafood in liquid. Add more liquid if seafood isn't covered.
- Continue simmering, uncovered, until seafood is cooked. Do not boil.

Microwave:

Microwave recipes in this book were developed using a 1200-watt microwave oven. Determine the wattage of your microwave oven since microwaves vary in the intensity of cooking power. Experiment to find the right cooking time for a particular recipe.

- Use the cooking guide of three minutes per pound of seafood.
- Arrange thicker pieces of seafood on the outside of the microwave proof dish for even cooking.
- Cover with microwave proof lid or microwave plastic wrap; leave a steam vent in plastic wrap .
- Estimate cooking time but check before recommended time has elapsed. You can always cook it more.

PEELING & DEVEINING SHRIMP

 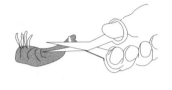 

Pull the head off where its armoring forms a natural division with the tail.

Peel off shell, leaving the legs, and cut lengthwise down the underside of the shrimp.

Pull the shell apart, removing the flesh.

Using a tweezers or toothpick, remove the vein from the center of the back.

To butterfly, cut along the back of the shrimp, but not all the way through. Spread the halves open.

CLEANING A SQUID

Under cold, running water, rub off the dark, thin skin with your fingers.

Remove the one bony part from within the sac.

Use your fingers to push out the hard beak (mouth parts) hidden in the center of the tentacles and snip these away; cut away the eyes.

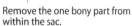 

Hold the main sac firmly and pull all the tentacles together away from the sac. Be careful not to break the ink sac.

How do I know when the fish is cooked?

Use a combination of temperature-time-texture-touch to determine when fish is cooked.

TEMPERATURE

The FDA recommends cooking fish until the internal temperature reaches 145°F. at the thickest part of the fish. Most chefs use a range of internal cooking temperatures, from 80°F. (seared tuna) to 140°F. When you have eaten and enjoyed a seafood dinner at a restaurant, ask the wait staff at what temperature the chef cooked your fish. Then go home and do it yourself. Remember: fish will continue to cook after it's been removed from the heat source.

TIME

The Canadian Department of Fisheries and Oceans recommends that fresh, thawed fish be cooked a total of 10 minutes per inch of thickness, measuring at the thickest part of the fish. This is based on a 450°F. oven pre-heated broiler or grill, and a medium-high fry pan.

**MEASURING
A FILLET**

**MEASURING A ROAST
OR WHOLE
FISH**

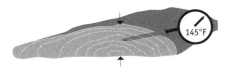

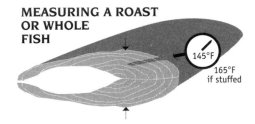

Measure fillet at thickest point. Cook 10 minutes per inch of thickness. To use thermometer, insert through side of fillet at thickest point.

Measure roast at thickest point. Cook 10 minutes per inch of thickness. To use thermometer, insert through side of roast at thickest point.

- Add five minutes if the fish is covered with vegetables or a sauce.
- Measure a fish after it is stuffed to determine thickness.
- Cooking it frozen—straight from the freezer—requires at least double the cooking time.

Microwave Cooking Tip

Microwave cooking times for seafood in a covered dish range from a total of 3 to 6 minutes per pound of boneless fish cooked on high (100% power), depending on the cooking power of your microwave.

DRESSING A LOBSTER

For lobster that is to be grilled, rather than boiled live, cut off legs near body.

Insert a knife in the abdomen, and cut through the under shell toward the head, leaving the back shell intact.

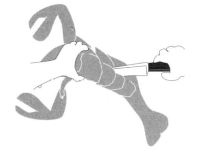

Cut toward the tail.

Press the lobster apart with your hands.

Remove the sand sac from the head; remove intestinal tract.

TEXTURE-TOUCH

Chefs use a combination of touching and seeing to determine when fish is cooked. Learn how to distinguish the feel of raw fish (bouncy) to the feel of cooked fish (firm) by lightly pressing a spatula on the fish fillet as it cooks. Exceptions to the rule are tuna, swordfish, marlin and shark. When raw, these species are naturally a firm texture. Monitoring their internal temperature with a thermometer is crucial. Salmon is a great fish to learn how to tell when it is cooked by the "look". A red sockeye salmon (raw) will turn a lighter orange-red color when done. Use your thermometer to test the internal temperature.

• Check the interior of the fish a few minutes before you expect it to be done.

- Use a thin-bladed knife to peek between the layers of flesh.
- When the fish is cooked, your knife will meet no resistance. Generally, the flesh is no longer translucent (like seeing through fine china) but, opaque (can't see through it).
- Remove it from the heat source the second it starts to flake or fall apart.
- Strategically plan your menu, working the cooking time backwards— foods with the longest cook-time go on the grill or in the oven first, food with the shortest cook-time go last.

How do I know when shellfish is cooked?

All shellfish is low fat and it cooks quickly.
- Clams, scallops and mussels in the shell will open when cooked. Some will need a gentle nudge if tightly closed.
- Shrimp shells will turn pink when cooked. Remove from heat source immediately.
- Lobster, Dungeness crab, blue crab, squid and clam meat cooks quickly.

How can I remove bones from my fish?

You can buy boneless fillets, but they usually cost more. Here's how to remove bones.
- Cut away pin bones with a sharp knife making a v-cut in the flesh.
- Pull bone from raw fish with tweezers.
- Cooked fish will shrink and bones will stick up from flesh. They can be easily seen and removed.

Will cooking seafood smell up my house?

Cooking good quality seafood should not stink up your home. If it does, then chances are the fish or shellfish is of poor quality. The kitchen should smell of herbs, spices and maybe a slight sea breeze. However, grilling outside, roasting seafood on a wood baking plank or in a Smoker Bag will help combat any smell. Some fish and shellfish naturally have a slightly more robust aroma. Your retailer can recommend a more pleasant smelling species.

Clean up immediately after cooking. Tightly wrap bones, skin, shells or package in a plastic bag. Discard in an outside garbage bin, freeze it until garbage day or dig in the garden to create a nutrient-rich soil. Immediately wash any dishes used in preparation, cooking or eating. Use the kitchen exhaust fan.

How do I save time cooking with seafood?

• Shop at stores that guarantee freshness at least three days after purchase. This eliminates every day shopping.

• Ask the seafood sales person for a quality recommendation and buy ahead for weekly planned meals.

• Save time by cooking two seafood meals at once, serving one immediately and refrigerating the second for lunch the next day.

• Stock up on frozen fish and shellfish.

• Select last-minute seafood salad ingredients from the supermarket such as bagged greens and ¼-lb of cooked crab or shrimp meat per person. Garnish salad with hard-boiled egg (from yesterday's breakfast), steamed asparagus, and some walnuts. Keep a stock of chilled salad garnishes in the refrigerator such as canned beets, olives, pickles and baby corn.

If you have more questions visit our web site at www.seafoodeducators.com.

Chapter 4

All About Seafood

I want to eat more seafood, but is it really safe?

You want to eat more seafood, and you want it to be safe and wholesome. The government, seafood industry, retailer and you share in the responsibility for ensuring the safety of the seafood that reaches your table. Your health has much to gain from eating more seafood. Experts agree, the health benefits from eating seafood far outweigh any risks.

What does the government do to keep seafood safe?

There are regulated layers of protection within the United States for all seafood products.

— **Federal:** The FDA inspects seafood processors, shippers, packers, labelers and retailers to assure that good quality, accurate labeling and sanitary handling procedures are maintained. If FDA standards aren't met, seafood will be recalled from being sold. The FDA also oversees the inspection program known as HACCP (Hazard Analysis and Critical Control Points) which requires every seafood processing facility to submit a plan for handling and monitoring critical control points where seafood safety risks are the greatest. Strict processing records are kept and the FDA monitors the implementation of these plans.

— **The National Shellfish Sanitation Program (NSSP)** is continually monitoring shellfish harvesting waters for the presence of pollutants and environmental contaminants. Shellfish that have received governmental approval will be labeled with a certification tag which identifies the time of harvest and location. Seafood shops, grocery stores and restaurants are required to make the tags available for your review. Just ask.

— **State:** The FDA sets action levels for a number of contaminants. State agencies are responsible for sampling suspected species. If contaminant levels exceed FDA limits, fishing of that species will be forbidden. This means it will not be sold to you, the consumer. These regulations are applied to recreational fishing and imported seafood, too. All foreign countries sign agreements to follow U.S. safety standards for seafood imported to the U.S.

— **Local:** Health departments are responsible for maintaining sanitation at grocery stores, restaurants, farmers' markets and fairs. This inspection process allows the consumer to stop at a roadside stand or dockside market with confidence because each vendor must be in compliance with the local officials. All sellers should have a current health card.

Should I be concerned about mercury in seafood?

The benefits of eating seafood "are likely to be at least 100-fold greater than the estimates of harm, which may not exist at all," according to Walter Willett, M.D., Professor of Nutrition at the Harvard School of Public Health. The science world is excited about a 16-year study in the Seychelles Islands. People there eat nearly 10 times the amount of seafood as Americans and about the same amount as fish-eating populations of Japan and Korea. As a result, the levels of mercury in their bodies are higher than ours. The offspring of Seychelles women who ate high-mercury fish diets while pregnant are completely healthy according to an announcement in February, 2006 by Dr. Davidson of the University of Rochester. "Not only did these children perform well on developmental tests, but they actually outperformed children whose mothers had eaten less fish." The elevated mercury levels appeared to have no negative effect on these children.

Because of the many nutritional benefits, women and young children particularly need to include fish or shellfish in their diets. According to an article in the American Journal of Preventive Medicine, eating less fish due to a fear of mercury will greatly increase a pregnant woman's risk of having an omega-3 deficiency in herself as well as in her unborn child.

The health advantages of eating seafood are acknowledged by almost all health and medical organizations. Eating fish at least two meals a week is recommended by the U.S. Dietary Guidelines, the American Heart Association, the National Academy of Sciences, the National Heart, Lung and Blood Institute and the American Diabetic Association.

The FDA and the Environmental Protection Agency (EPA) state that for most people, the risk from mercury by eating seafood is not a health concern. Women who may become pregnant, pregnant women, nursing women and young children, are advised to consume 12 ounces of a variety of seafood weekly (4 servings) but avoid swordfish, shark, king mackerel and tilefish.

Call the FDA at 1-888-Safefood or visit the FDA website at www.cfsan.fda.gov or www.epa.gov for current seafood advisories.

Did you know?
William Lands, M.D., *retired from the National Institute of Health, says, "Nearly all seafood contains selenium. Selenium in seafood counteracts any trend toward mercury having a toxic effect."*

What about seafood allergies?

While research continues on food allergies, Artemis P. Simopoulos, M.D., suggests creating a "smart" immune system. Medical researchers are beginning to treat immune disorders, such as allergies, with a balanced diet of omega-3s to omega-6s.

The true prevalence of seafood allergies is estimated to be less than 2 percent of the US population. They are most commonly associated with adults.

The 8 most common food allergens are: milk and other

dairy, eggs, peanuts, tree nuts (walnuts, cashews, etc), fish, shellfish, soy and soy products and wheat. These foods must be listed on the ingredient label.

Read ingredient labels carefully. Talk to your health care provider or visit American Academy of Allergy, Asthma and Immunology at www.aaaai.org for updated information.

Is there enough seafood to keep us healthy?

There is no question that we are stewards of our seas, rivers and lakes which are on loan to us. No one wants to eat the last fish. Global attention is being paid to the sustainability of farmed and wild seafood, including the environmental, social and economic impacts of eating more seafood. The Marine Stewardship Council, a London-based, independent non-profit organization, certifies sustainable seafood. Look for their label on packaged seafood or at the seafood counter and visit their web site, www.MSC.org. The Monterey Bay Aquarium's Seafood Watch program encourages chefs and retailers to make sustainable seafood choices. They suggest "Best Choices" such as replacing Atlantic cod with Pacific cod or pollock and reducing selected farmed salmon or shrimp purchases. Visit their web site at www.seafoodwatch.org

Aquaculture is one alternative to keeping the world's supply supporting the demand. Worldwide production of seafood from farms and aquaculture operations is growing more rapidly than production of all other food-producing animals.

According to the 2006 annual National Oceanic and Atmospheric Administration (NOAA) report, 74% of major wild U.S. fisheries assessed are not considered over-fished and 81% are not currently subject to over-fishing. NOAA assesses all major stocks that are targeted by commercial and recreational fisheries.

Retailers and restaurant owners are developing their own definition of sustainable seafood. Many are asking for complete traceability from water to table and will make purchase decisions based on the accountability.

What is the difference between farmed and wild seafood?

Seafood comes from two distinct and different production sources: farmed and wild.

Farmed seafood is a hybrid of traditional fishing and agriculture. The seafood crop is dependent on tidal waters or fish pellets for food. Abalone, oysters, mussels and clams receive sustaining nutrients from the tidal waters as they have for thousands of years. The environment they grow in determines color, flavor, texture and meatiness. Farmed seafood such as salmon, tilapia, catfish, trout and shrimp are raised in ponds or tanks located in the ocean or on land. The contents of the manufactured pellets and water composition will determine the nutritional profile, flesh color, texture, oil content and taste of the seafood.

Wild seafood will naturally have distinguishing features of texture, color, flavor and nutrient profile. The feed, environment and harvesting location determines some of their quality, taste and nutrient levels.

Wild shellfish taste and texture profile will reflect the water composition they live in. For instance, the Eastern oyster is known for its distinctive, salty flavor and meaty texture. The Pacific Northwest oysters are mild and sweet, with a briny flavor and crisp texture.

Taste, meat texture, color and nutritional value for both farmed and wild seafood depend on the feeding location, time of year and harvest techniques.

Many retailers are requiring complete transparency and traceability on the life of seafood they are selling. They know the composition of the feed and water, the location, time and technique of harvest. Retailers are setting quality standards by requiring specific techniques and temperatures for processing, handling and distribution.

Did you know?

FDA labeling laws require a prominent display at the point of purchase naming the country of origin and if the seafood is farmed or wild. Currently under review, FDA does not allow either farmed or wild seafood to be labeled organic.

I love raw oysters. Is it safe for me to eat them?

Americans have a passion for raw oysters. Most of these mollusks are considered safe to eat raw for the majority of healthy individuals. When harvested from approved waters, and handled under a HACCP plan, the potential for illness is minimal.

On the other hand, the FDA considers some consumers to be at high risk because of specific medical conditions and states that such individuals should never consume raw oysters. People at highest risk are those with liver disease or who have compromised immune systems from other diseases, such as AIDS, chronic alcohol abuse, stomach or blood disorders, cancer, diabetes and kidney disease. Individuals with these health conditions should eat oysters fully cooked. If you are in good health and know the source of the oysters, continue enjoying raw oysters without undue concern.

Is all sushi raw?

No! Sushi is simply a Japanese staple, made with seasoned rice and seafood. Sometimes it is seaweed-wrapped with beautifully cut, raw vegetables inside. Sushi chefs can offer varieties that are made with cooked shrimp, surimi, tuna or smoked salmon or raw seafood. Several school districts across the country are now serving fully cooked sushi using wild Alaskan pouched salmon and it's quickly becoming a lunch time favorite.

What is sashimi?

Sashimi is raw, thinly sliced fish and shellfish. Because it is very delicate, it is considered the seafood of royalty. A sushi/sashimi chef receives years of training to learn quality standards and cutting skills to serve perfect sashimi.

The chef asks for and receives the entire genealogy record of the fish starting from the moment it was caught to the hour it was purchased. Included in the record is the time of year, harvesting technique, fat content and temperature control. Their learned skills give them confidence to serve frozen sashimi seafood, too. These chefs only become successful when customers return. Their reputation is a sign of honor.

The interest in sashimi has increased the demand for live seafood. Chinese and Japanese restaurants and supermarkets have always carried live seafood. Now supermarkets across the United States are installing live fish and shellfish tanks to guarantee freshness and to support the sashimi interest. Eating sashimi will reveal how tasty all seafood can be.

What questions should I ask at the seafood counter?

Like the sashimi chef, the seafood business survives on repeat, satisfied customers who trust them. Ask the retailer the following questions:
1. Would you serve this to your family?
2. What do you recommend I cook for my family today?
3. Are there certain days of the week when the seafood is freshest?
4. What is your quality guarantee?

What do I need to do at home to keep seafood safe and from spoiling?

1. **Consider safety...when bringing it home:**
   - Shop for your seafood at the end of your trip.
   - Make sure your purchase is tightly wrapped.
   - Keep separate from other raw or cooked meats.
   - Ice package or use a cooler for transportation.
2. **Consider safety...in storage:**
   - Refrigerate fresh seafood immediately in the coldest section of your refrigerator. Keep refrigerator temperature between 32° and 38° F.
   - Fresh seafood should be cooked in 1-2 days. If you plan to consume your seafood later in the week, freeze it immediately to maintain quality.
   - Cooked, refrigerated seafood can be held for 3-4 days (if YOU cooked it). If you bought it cooked, refrigerate it for 1-2 days.
   - Rotate cans and jars in your pantry so that the oldest items are used first.
3. **Consider safety...in preparation:**
   Remember: Cleanliness is the key! The most common cause of seafood-related illnesses in the home is due to

cross-contamination.

Cross-contamination occurs when raw seafood or seafood juices come into contact with cooked seafood or any other food that will not be cooked.

Cross-contamination can be easily avoided if raw seafood is kept separate from cooked in the refrigerator. Store raw seafood in a water proof container with a tight lid. Live shellfish (such as mussels or clams) should be stored in a water proof container, covered with a breathable paper or fabric. They should be used within 2-3 days. Oysters in the shell can be refrigerated for up to seven days.

- Wash! Wash! Wash! Wash hands thoroughly. Use hot, soapy water. Wash for at least 20 seconds.
  Wash hands repeatedly:
    - Before handling seafood
    - After using the bathroom
    - After sneezing
    - After touching raw seafood or seafood juices
- Thoroughly wash knives, cutting boards, kitchen counters and hands when working from raw to cooked foods.
- Thoroughly cook anything that comes into contact with seafood or seafood juices.
- Be a kitchen germ detective! Follow the germ trail in your home--from packaging to plate, brush, utensil, and sink. Change sponges frequently and wipe down work surfaces with diluted bleach or other disinfectants. Don't give germs and bacteria a chance to grow.
- Prepare raw seafood in a designated area - separate from other food preparation. Handle raw seafood away from foods that have been cooked or will be consumed without cooking. A spot near the sink works well. Keep everything used to prepare raw seafood in that area.
- Whenever possible, handle seafood last--after fruit and salads are stored in the refrigerator and sliced bread set aside.
- Use a separate cutting board for raw seafood. Sprinkle with cleanser, detergent or immediately put in dishwasher after using. Clean thoroughly.
- Whenever preparing raw seafood, fill a sink with hot soapy water. When finished using an item, immediately place it in the soapy water. This will

reduce the temptation to reuse dishes, knives and utensils. Remember to keep the water hot.

4. Consider safety...in cooking:

- Cook fish for 10 minutes per inch of thickness, measuring at the thickest point until the internal temperature reaches 145° F. Generally, this internal temperature has been reached when the fish loses its translucency and flakes when tested with a fork.
- Oysters, clams and mussels in the shell should be steamed 4-6 minutes after the liquid returns to a boil. Steaming shellfish in small batches will allow heat to better penetrate the flesh.
- Hot-smoking seafood will kill parasites if the internal temperature of the thickest portion is held at 145°F. for a minimum of 10 seconds.

5. Consider safety...in cleanup:

- Refrigerate leftover seafood as soon as possible after eating. Any cooked seafood left at room temperature for two hours or more should be discarded.
- Thoroughly wash cutting boards and utensils after preparing seafood.
- Clean countertops.
- Sanitize sinks with cleanser.
- Wash your dishcloth or sponge after each seafood meal is prepared.

REMEMBER: The majority of seafood illness is associated with: Sport caught or uninspected seafood from contaminated waters.
— Raw or undercooked seafood, especially oysters, clams, and mussels.
— Contamination by improper handling in the home.

Follow these suggestions and enjoy many delicious seafood meals to come!

Chapter 5

Appetizers

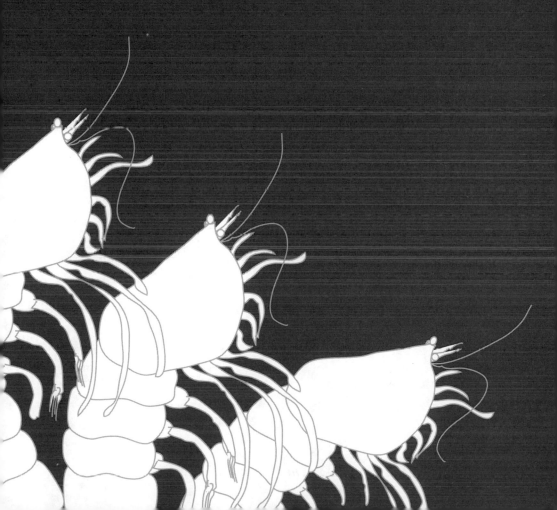

$100 Salmon Cheese Ball

It's true! A friend's aunt asked a restaurant chef for this recipe. The chef took her name and address and mailed her this recipe and an invoice. Aunt Teresa was so mad she took him to court and lost. Now, she wants everyone in the whole-wide world to enjoy this recipe.

Prep Time	Cook Time	Yields
5-10 minutes	None	48 T. (3 C.)

1	7 oz. can salmon, boneless, skinless, drained, flaked
1	8 oz. pkg. low-fat cream cheese
4 oz.	blue cheese
1	10 oz. jar cheddar cheese spread
2 T.	onion, minced
1	garlic clove, minced
1 tsp.	Worcestershire sauce
½ tsp.	crushed red pepper flakes
½ C.	pecans, chopped
½ C.	fresh parsley, chopped

1. Blend the cheeses in a bowl until smooth.
2. Add salmon, onion, garlic, Worcestershire and red pepper flakes. Mix well.
3. Shape into 3 balls. Roll in pecans and parsley.
4. Cover. Refrigerate. Serve.

Substitutions: Smoked salmon, canned tuna, crab meat

Tip: *Allow the cheeses to come to room temperature. Or microwave for about 20 seconds to soften.*

Nutrients Per Tablespoon:

Calories	80
Omega-3s	97mg
Total Fat	7g
Saturated Fat	4g
Protein	4g
Total Carbohydrate	1g
Cholesterol	15mg
Sodium	150mg
Fiber	0g

Ceviche Cocktail

Traditional ceviche calls for raw seafood to cook in fresh lemon or lime juice. I prefer to marinate cooked seafood with traditional ceviche ingredients.

Prep Time	Cook Time	Yields
10 minutes	None	8 servings

1 lb.	cooked shrimp meat, peeled, deveined
½ C.	ketchup
¼ C.	orange juice
¼ C.	lime juice
1½ tsp.	Worcestershire sauce
½ tsp.	hot sauce
1	small onion, diced
¼ C.	red bell pepper, diced
¼ C.	green bell pepper, diced
3	Roma tomatoes, diced
2	jalapeño chilies, seeded, diced
½ C.	cilantro, minced
2	ripe avocados, peeled, diced

Tip: Vary the flavors using lemon juice, sushi vinegar, Mexican oregano, garlic, chipotle or poblano chilies, capers and olives.

1. Mix ketchup, orange and lime juices, Worcestershire and hot sauce in a non-aluminum bowl. Add shrimp and remaining ingredients except avocado.
2. Cover bowl. Refrigerate.
3. To serve, drain liquid. Cube avocados and gently mix with shrimp. Season with salt and pepper to taste. Arrange in pre-chilled cocktail glasses or onto salad plates.

Substitutions: crab meat, surimi, poached bay scallops

Nutrients Per Serving:

Calories	172
Omega-3s	523mg
Total Fat	5g
Saturated Fat	1g
Protein	21g
Total Carbohydrate	0
Cholesterol	57mg
Sodium	310mg
Fiber	3g

Shrimp Kebobs with Cilantro Basil Sauce

Prep Time	Cook Time	Yields
15-minutes	None	8-10 servings

1 lb.   cooked shrimp, medium large
Small appetizer picks or wooden skewers

Cilantro Basil Sauce
4 T.   fresh orange juice
2 T.   light mayonnaise
1 C.   cilantro
½ C.   basil leaves
½ C.   parsley
1   serrano chili pepper, seeded
salt and pepper, to taste

1. Place all sauce ingredients in a blender or food processor. Process until the mixture is a pulpy pureé. Season sauce to taste.
2. Refrigerate several hours or overnight. (Use within 24 hours.)

Fruits and vegetables, such as:
1   red bell pepper, cut into 1-inch squares
1   8 oz. can pineapple chunks, drained
½ C.   cantaloupe chunks
½ C.   honeydew chunks
½ C.   strawberries

1. Thread shrimp, fruits, vegetables on small appetizer picks or 6-inch wooden skewers, roughly 4 shrimp per skewer. The skewers can be made ahead, covered and refrigerated.
2. Serve with Sauce.

Substitutions: cooked scallops or lobster meat

Nutrients Per Kebob:

Calories	100
Omega-3s	215mg
Total Fat	1g
Saturated Fat	0g
Protein	12g
Total Carbohydrate	10g
Cholesterol	10mg
Sodium	131mg
Fiber	2g

Chipotle Salsa Crab Dip

A Super Bowl Favorite

Prep Time	Cook Time	Yields
5-10 minutes	None	32 T. (2 C.)

1 lb.	surimi, chopped
8 oz.	low-fat cream cheese, softened
1 C.	extra chunky salsa
1 tsp.	canned chipotle in adobo sauce

1. Blend softened cream cheese in a bowl with a fork until smooth.
2. Add surimi, salsa and chipotle.
3. Refrigerate for several hours or overnight.
4. Serve with toasted whole wheat baguettes, or vegetable tray

Tip: *Remove cream cheese from refrigerator an hour before preparing dish, or microwave until soft.*

Substitutions: cooked, chopped crab, shrimp, lobster meat, canned salmon, tuna

Nutrients Per Tablespoon:

Calories	34
Omega-3s	101mg
Total Fat	2g
Saturated Fat	1g
Protein	2g
Total Carbohydrate	2g
Cholesterol	10mg
Sodium	160mg
Fiber	0g

Fantastic Salmon Quesadillas

Prep Time	Cook Time	Yields
5-10 minutes	10 minutes	4 servings

1	7 oz. can or pouched salmon, drained, flaked
1	4 oz. can green chilies, drained or 1 red chili pepper, sliced
4	whole wheat flour tortillas
1 C.	Monterey jack cheese, grated

vegetable cooking spray

Garnish with salsa, light sour cream, or guacamole

1. Mix salmon and chilies.
2. Spread two tortillas with the salmon mixture and cheese.
3. Top each with remaining tortillas.
4. Lightly spray heated frying pan.
5. Lay a quesadilla in the pan. Brown both sides, melting cheese.
6. Remove to a plate and keep warm.
7. Repeat with the other quesadilla.
8. Slice quesadillas in quarters and serve with garnish if desired.

Nutrients Per Serving:

Calories	262
Omega-3s	603mg
Total Fat	13g
Saturated Fat	6g
Protein	16g
Total Carbohydrate	19g
Cholesterol	40mg
Sodium	614mg
Fiber	2g

Seafood Puffs

These party favorites are simple to make and very impressive.

Prep Time	Cook Time	Yields
20-25 minutes	approx. 45 min. total	8-10 Servings

Filling

1	6 oz. can Albacore tuna, drained
2 T.	celery, finely chopped
¼ tsp.	Worcestershire sauce
2 T.	low-fat mayonnaise

Puffs

1 C.	low-fat milk
½ C.	butter
1 C.	flour
¼ tsp.	salt
4	large eggs

For Puffs

1. Preheat oven to 400°F. Grease a cookie sheet.
2. Boil milk and butter in a medium sized sauce pan over medium heat.
3. Add flour and salt. Quickly stir.
4. Dough will become smooth. When it stops sticking to sides of pan or spoon, remove from heat. If dough cooks too long it won't puff. Cool.
5. Add one egg at a time into dough, mixing each egg for 2 minutes.
6. Drop dough in tablespoon-sized dollops onto a cookie sheet.
7. Bake at 400°F. for 10 minutes. Reduce heat to 350°F. Bake 30 minutes longer, or until puffs are quite firm.
8. Remove from oven and poke a hole in the side of each puff with a knife, return to oven for 4 more minutes.
9. Remove from oven and cool before filling.

For Filling

1. Mix filling ingredients while the puffs are baking.
2. As close to serving time as possible, pull each cream puff in half and fill with a teaspoon full of filling.

Substitutions: cooked salmon, crab, lobster or shrimp meat

Tip: *Bake puffs a day ahead and seal in an air tight bag.*

Nutrients Per Puff:

Calories	38
Omega-3s	103mg
Total Fat	3g
Saturated Fat	2g
Protein	6g
Total Carbohydrate	2g
Cholesterol	20mg
Sodium	60mg
Fiber	1g

Seared Tuna Sashimi
with Teriyaki Sauce

Prep Time	Cook Time	Yields
5-10 minutes	4 minutes	4 servings

1 lb.   ahi tuna
canola oil

Teriyaki Sauce
½ C.   soy sauce
½ C.   brown sugar
2 T.   white wine
1½ T.   fresh parsley, chopped
1½ tsp. fresh ginger root, peeled, minced
1½ tsp. garlic, minced
½ tsp.   fresh lemon juice

1. Mix all sauce ingredients in a jar or medium bowl.
2. Cover and refrigerate for several hours to blend flavors.
3. Shake or stir well before using.
4. Pre-heat grill.
5. Lightly coat both sides of tuna with canola oil.
6. Place tuna on grill and sear for 3 minutes. Turn. Sear for 1 minute.
7. Slice thin and fan tuna out on plate. Serve with teriyaki sauce.

Substitutions: marlin, swordfish, shark

Tip: Use a sushi or mild vinegar instead of white wine.

Nutrients Per Serving:

Calories	177
Omega-3s	268mg
Total Fat	7g
Saturated Fat	2g
Protein	26g
Total Carbohydrate	50g
Cholesterol	43mg
Sodium	214 mg
Fiber	1g

Smoked Seafood Party Platter

Omega-3 content is not changed when seafood is smoked, canned, frozen, or cooked. Interestingly, it's the high-fat fish that is usually smoked, making it a nutritional keeper.

Lox, Nova Scotia or Nova style, or cold smoked seafoods are lightly salted with or without added sugar, herbs or brines. Traditionally, these products have the lowest salt content of all smoked seafood. The meat is very moist, has a firm, yet tender texture with a mild smoky flavor.

Kippered, hot smoked seafood is smoked and fully cooked seafood with the internal temperature reaching 145°F.for 30 minutes. It contains less moisture and usually has a stronger smoke flavor. The meat may have added flavors such as garlic, teriyaki, cracked pepper, or Cajun.

Dried or jerky seafood is salted and smoked at a low temperature for a long time to remove moisture. The texture is chewy like beef jerky. Kids love it.

Herbed Cream Cheese

1	8 oz. pkg. low-fat cream cheese
2 T.	low-fat milk
2 tsp.	each lemon juice, horseradish sauce
2 tsp.	dill weed
4-5	drops hot pepper sauce

1. Beat all ingredients until smooth. Serve in a small bowl.
2. Arrange a decorative tray with a variety of smoked seafood. Serve with herbed cream cheese, capers, thinly sliced red onion, bagels, pumpernickel bread, or crackers.

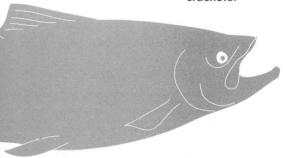

Smoked Salmon Finger Sushi

In the early 1990s, I introduced salmon sushi into schools across America. At first the school cooks thought I was crazy, but several districts gave it a try. The sushi lunch line grew in popularity so fast that one school bought mechanical sushi making machines and still couldn't keep up with the demand. We can teach our kids to enjoy seafood!

Prep Time	Cook Time	Yields
5-10 minutes	35 minutes	12 servings (¾ C.)

8 oz. smoked salmon, sliced nova style lox
Wasabi (Japanese horseradish)
sliced, pickled ginger

Sushi Rice
1 C.   sushi rice, (short grain Japanese rice)
1½ C.   water

1. Wash rice under cold running water until water becomes clear.
2. In a deep pot, soak rice with just enough water to cover kernels. Cover and refrigerate at least 30 minutes.
3. Drain water from rice. Add 1½ cups of water. Put lid on pot.
4. Cook over medium heat until water boils. When it begins to boil, cook for 1 minute.
5. Turn heat to low for 15 minutes.
6. Turn off heat and let rice stand for 10 minutes.

Rice Seasoning
2 T.   sushi rice vinegar

1. Put cooked rice in a shallow mixing bowl.
2. Sprinkle sushi vinegar evenly over rice.
3. Mix, using a folding motion with a spoon or paddle. Use a hand fan or electric fan to remove extra moisture. This will help puff the extra liquid away.

recipe continued ☞

Tip: *Dip sushi seafood side only, into sauce. Do not dip the rice side into sauce, as it will fall apart.*

Nutrition Per Sushi:

Calories	40
Omega-3s	90mg
Total Fat	3g
Saturated Fat	0g
Protein	2g
Total Carbohydrate	2g
Cholesterol	0mg
Sodium	285mg
Fiber	0g

–Recipe continued–

To Make Finger Sushi:
1. Take a heaping tablespoon of rice in your left hand between your thumb and first finger. Using right hand thumb and first finger, shape the rice into an oblong. Press, squeeze and mold until rice is about 1½" long.
2. Lightly spread with wasabi. Put salmon on top of rice.
3. Serve with pickled ginger.

Sushi or Sashimi Balsamic Honey and Thyme Dipping Sauce

Prep Time	Cook Time	Yields
5-10 minutes	None	12 T. (¾ C.)

¼ C.	balsamic vinegar
¼ C.	honey
¼ C.	olive oil
2 T.	fresh thyme, minced
2 tsp.	kosher salt
½ tsp.	black pepper
½ tsp.	garlic, minced

Nutrients Per Tablespoon:

Calories	70
Omega-3s	38mg
Total Fat	5g
Saturated Fat	1g
Protein	0g
Total Carbohydrate	8g
Cholesterol	0mg
Sodium	390mg
Fiber	0g

1. Mix all ingredients in a jar or bowl.
2. Cover and refrigerate for several hours to allow flavors to blend.
3. Shake or stir well before serving.
4. Uncover bowl or put sauce into a serving bowl.
5. Serve with sushi, sashimi or kebobs.

Smoky Salmon Cream Cheese Spread

Many of our daughter's teachers received this for a holiday thank-you gift. They loved having something homemade on hand for entertaining.

Prep Time	Cook Time	Yields
5-10 minutes	None	24 T. (1½ C.)

1	**7 oz. can sockeye salmon, boneless, skinless, drained**
1	**8 oz. pkg. low-fat cream cheese**
3 drops	**liquid smoke flavoring**
1½ tsp.	**fresh lemon juice**
1 tsp.	**horseradish (optional)**
3 T.	**green onion, sliced**
¼ C.	**nuts, chopped**
¼ C.	**parsley, chopped**

1. Mix all ingredients except nuts and parsley in a bowl.
2. Refrigerate for several hours to blend flavors.
3. Roll in parsley or crushed nuts to make salmon cheese balls or logs.
4. Serve an impressive appetizer tray by filling celery sticks, hollowed-out cherry tomatoes, or hard-boiled eggs (yolks removed), or top cucumber slices or toasted party bagels with spread.

Substitutions: cooked albacore tuna, crab or clam meat

Nutrients Per Tablespoon:

Calories	35
Omega-3s	140mg
Total Fat	3g
Saturated Fat	2g
Protein	2g
Total Carbohydrate	0g
Cholesterol	10mg
Sodium	75mg
Fiber	1g

Spicy Shrimp Skewers

Prep Time	Cook Time	Yields
5-10 minutes	about 10 minutes	6 servings

1 lb.	raw shrimp, peeled, deveined
1 T.	olive oil
1 T.	butter
6	12" bamboo skewers, cut in half

Marinade

¼ C.	fresh lime juice, from about 2 limes
2 T.	canola oil
2 tsp.	ground cumin
2 tsp.	ground coriander
1 tsp.	cayenne pepper
1 tsp.	turmeric
1 tsp.	ground cardamom
½ tsp.	garlic powder
½ tsp.	ground cinnamon
¼ tsp.	salt

1. Mix marinade in a glass pan.
2. Thread shrimp onto skewers.
3. Place skewers in marinade. Cover. Refrigerate for 4 hours, turning occasionally.
4. After shrimp have marinated, save the marinade.
5. Heat olive oil and butter in a large frying pan. Sauté skewers for about 2 minutes on each side, or until they are completely pink.
6. Remove skewers and keep warm on a serving platter.
7. Add marinade to frying pan and boil for at least 5 minutes.
8. Drizzle this over the cooked shrimp, serve with bread to dip into the sauce.

Substitutions: scallops

Nutrients Per Skewer:

Calories	134
Omega-3s	802mg
Total Fat	6g
Saturated Fat	1g
Protein	16g
Total Carbohydrate	4g
Cholesterol	115mg
Sodium	114mg
Fiber	1g

Stuffed Tomatoes with Shrimp

Prep Time	Cook Time	Yields
5-10 minutes	None	8-10 servings

Stuffing

½ lb.	cooked salad shrimp, chopped
½ C.	low-fat cream cheese, softened
1 T.	Mrs. Dash Original Blend or Italian seasoning
1 T.	fresh lemon juice
⅓ C.	crushed, canned, unsweetened pineapple, thoroughly drained
2 T.	walnuts, finely chopped
¼ tsp.	salt
⅛ tsp.	Tabasco sauce, to taste

Vegetables

15	cherry tomatoes - or -
3	celery stalks, cut into 2-inch pieces - or -
1	English cucumber, sliced - or -
	bell pepper strips

dash of paprika

1. Mix stuffing ingredients in a bowl.
2. Fill tomatoes (or other vegetable listed) with stuffing.
3. Garnish with paprika.
4. Arrange on a serving platter.

Substitutions: canned salmon or crab meat, surimi

Tip: *Garnish with caviar for an Omega-3-packed appetizer.*

Nutrients Per Serving:

Calories	80
Omega-3s	292mg
Total Fat	5g
Saturated Fat	3g
Protein	8g
Total Carbohydrate	1g
Cholesterol	65mg
Sodium	170mg
Fiber	0g

Stuffed Eggs with Seafood

Prep Time	Cook Time	Yields
20 minutes	10 minutes	12 servings

1	6.5 oz. can smoked salmon
12	eggs, hard-cooked, shells removed
½ C.	low-fat mayonnaise
½ C.	parsley, minced
3 T.	lemon juice
1 T.	Dijon mustard
¼ tsp.	ground pepper
¼ tsp.	cayenne pepper
1 tsp.	chives, chopped, garnish

Tip: *Prepare filling and stuff eggs up to 4 hours before serving. Cover. Refrigerate.*

1. Hard cook eggs a day ahead, leave shells on. Cover. Store in refrigerator.
2. Shell eggs. Cut hard cooked eggs lengthwise in half with a sharp knife. Remove yolks and set whites on serving platter.
3. Mix 6 yolks with mayonnaise, parsley, lemon juice, Dijon mustard, ground and cayenne pepper. (Add sardines or chopped, smoked oyster if substituting seafood.) Mash and mix with a fork.
4. Spoon filling into egg whites halves, dividing it evenly among eggs.
5. Top filled eggs with smoked salmon. Garnish with chives.

Substitutions: cooked salad shrimp, smoked kippers or oysters, caviar

Nutrients Per Serving:

Calories	43
Omega-3s	78mg
Total Fat	6g
Saturated Fat	2g
Protein	13g
Total Carbohydrate	2g
Cholesterol	71mg
Sodium	210mg
Fiber	0g

Party Crab Bites

Prep Time	Cook Time	Yields
10 minutes	12 minutes	36 bites

8 oz.	crab meat
1½ C.	bread crumbs
1	egg, beaten
2 T.	low-fat mayonnaise
2 T.	cocktail sauce
2 T.	green onion, minced
1 tsp.	dried parsley, chopped
½ tsp.	dry mustard
dash	cayenne pepper
dash	black pepper
1C.	corn flakes, crushed

1. Mix all ingredients except corn flakes in a large bowl.
2. Cover. Chill for 1 hour or overnight.
3. Preheat oven to 425°F.
4. Form crab mixture into ball using a teaspoon for each bite. Roll crab in crushed corn flakes. Place on oiled baking sheet.
5. Bake for 10 to 12 minutes or until golden brown.
6. Serve with cocktail sauce.

Substitutions: lobster, shrimp meat, surimi (imitation crab)

Tip: *Crab mixture may be used as a stuffing for mushrooms or baked in an oven proof serving dish. Top with corn flakes.*

Nutrients Per Serving:

Calories	30
Omega-3s	70mg
Total Fat	1g
Saturated Fat	1g
Protein	3g
Total Carbohydrate	5g
Cholesterol	12mg
Sodium	78mg
Fiber	1g

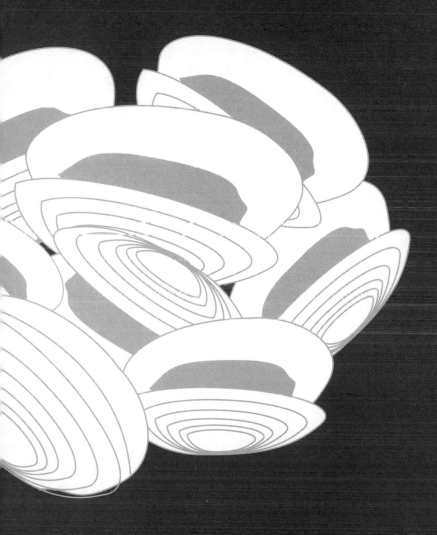

Chapter 6

Soups

Asian Noodle Soup

This soup is very quick — good for lunch when you're hungry. Experiment with noodles from the international food aisle.

Prep Time	Cook Time	Yields
5-10 minutes	15-20 minutes	4 servings

1 C.	surimi (imitation crab)
1 tsp.	olive oil
1 C.	onion, chopped
1	celery stalk, sliced, 4 celery tops with leaves, if available
½ tsp.	garlic, minced
⅛ tsp.	ground ginger
⅛ tsp.	crushed red pepper flakes
4 C.	water
1 cube	chicken bouillon
2 oz.	Asian noodles (buckwheat soba, bean threads, rice vermicelli)
⅛ tsp.	sesame oil, or to taste
¼ C.	green onions, chopped

1. Heat olive oil in a 2-quart saucepan; add onion, celery, garlic, ginger, pepper flakes. Stir.
2. Turn heat to low, cover, sweat vegetables for 5 minutes.
3. Add water, bouillon, reserved celery leaves. Bring to a boil. Stir.
4. Add noodles and reduce heat to simmer for time specified on the package. Add surimi and sesame oil. Heat until just hot.
5. Fill bowls with soup, giving each bowl a celery top. Garnish with green onions.

Substitutions: cooked, peeled shrimp, squid

Tip: *Sweating vegetables intensifies the flavor and keeps the vegetables more moist.*

Nutrients Per Serving:

Calories	112
Omega-3s	177mg
Total Fat	2g
Saturated Fat	0g
Protein	6g
Total Carbohydrate	19g
Cholesterol	6mg
Sodium	543mg
Fiber	2g

Autumn Fish Stew

Fishermen traditionally use their day's catch, seasonal herbs, spices and vegetables to make (perhaps) the worlds' first comfort food.

Prep Time	Cook Time	Yields
10-15 minutes	45-50 minutes	4 servings

1 lb.	halibut, cut into 1-inch cubes
1	medium onion, chopped
2 T.	olive oil
1	28 oz. can seasoned tomatoes, undrained
2	medium potatoes, peeled, diced
½ tsp.	dried basil
¼ tsp.	black pepper
¼ tsp.	crushed red pepper flakes
1	10 oz. package frozen mixed vegetables

1. In a 4-quart saucepan, sauté onion in oil until tender.
2. Stir in the undrained tomatoes.
3. Add potatoes, basil, pepper, red pepper flakes and vegetables. Heat until boiling.
4. Reduce heat to low. Cover. Simmer 20 minutes, stirring occasionally.
5. Add fish and simmer 5 minutes.
6. Serve with crusty bread.

Substitutions: shrimp, grouper, cod

Nutrients Per Serving:

Calories	203
Omega-3s	400mg
Total Fat	6g
Saturated Fat	1g
Protein	21g
Total Carbohydrate	42g
Cholesterol	27mg
Sodium	375mg
Fiber	5g

Bouillabaisse

Prep Time	Cook Time	Yields
15-20 minutes	30-35 minutes	6 servings

2 lbs.	a variety of seafood: white-fleshed fish, shrimp, scallops, oysters, crab, clams, mussels
¼ C.	olive oil
1	onion, sliced into thin rings
1	garlic clove, minced
2	large fresh tomatoes, coarsely chopped
¼ C.	fresh parsley, chopped
1 tsp.	salt
1	bay leaf
½ tsp.	dried oregano
½ tsp.	crushed red pepper flakes
¼ tsp.	dried thyme
2 C.	fish stock or water
1 C.	white wine or chicken stock

1. Prepare seafood: cut fish into 1-inch pieces, shell shrimp, scrub clam and mussel shells.
2. Heat olive oil in a 4-quart saucepan; sauté onion, garlic, tomatoes, parsley, seasonings for 5 minutes.
3. Cover, bring to a boil, reduce heat and simmer for 10 minutes.
4. Place fish and shellfish in saucepan. Add wine and fish stock.
5. Cover saucepan. Bring to a boil. Reduce heat and simmer for 10 minutes.
6. Serve with a thick slice of crusty French bread.

Tip: *If using surimi (imitation crab), add in the last 2 minutes of cooking.*

Nutrients Per Serving:

Calories	258
Omega-3s	466mg
Total Fat	11g
Saturated Fat	2g
Protein	25g
Total Carbohydrate	9g
Cholesterol	130mg
Sodium	516mg
Fiber	1g

Evie's Razor Clam Chowder

I grew up digging razor clams. They are a sweet Northwest delicacy that is worth braving the cold wind and rain.

Prep Time	Cook Time	Yields
5-10 minutes	20-21 minutes	4 servings

1 lb.	fresh, canned or frozen clam meat, minced
1	sweet onion, chopped
3	stalks celery, chopped
4	red potatoes, cubed
2	carrots, sliced
1½ tsp.	Italian seasoning
1 tsp.	salt
¼ tsp.	white pepper
¼ tsp.	garlic powder
¼ tsp.	nutmeg
2 C.	water
2 C.	heavy cream
1 T.	flour
1 T.	parsley, chopped (optional)
dash	hot sauce

Tip: *To make Manhattan Clam Chowder, substitute a 28 oz. can of mashed tomatoes with juice, for the cream.*

1. Add clam meat, onion, celery, potatoes, carrots, spices, water in a saucepan. Stir. Cover.
2. Cook on low heat until tender, about 15 minutes.
3. Mix cream and flour in a small bowl. Pour into clam base in saucepan. Bring to a boil, reduce heat and simmer for 5 minutes. Stir.
4. Garnish with chopped parsley, if you like.
5. Serve immediately.

Substitutions: scallops, salmon, lobster

Nutrients Per Serving:

Calories	322
Omega-3s	205mg
Total Fat	6g
Saturated Fat	3g
Protein	26g
Total Carbohydrate	45g
Cholesterol	51mg
Sodium	552mg
Fiber	5g

Gilbert's Mom's Fish Soup

Gilbert sells seafood in Santa Monica, California and proudly shares his mother's recipes with his customers!

Prep Time	Cook Time	Yields
5-10 minutes	15-20 minutes	4 servings

1 lb.	white-fleshed fish, such as cod or rockfish, cut into 2-inch pieces
1 T.	butter
1 C.	brown rice
3	fresh tomatoes, skinned, chopped
3 C.	tomato-based vegetable juice, such as V8
1 tsp.	salt
1 tsp.	paprika
1 tsp.	black pepper
1 tsp.	Tabasco, or to taste
3 T.	fresh lemon juice

1. Melt butter over medium heat in a 2-quart saucepan.
2. Add rice and cook, stirring constantly, until rice turns golden brown.
3. Stir in tomatoes, vegetable juice, salt, paprika, pepper, Tabasco.
4. Simmer on low heat, covered, for 10 minutes. Stir occasionally.
5. Add lemon juice and fish, stir, simmer for 10 minutes more, until rice is soft and fish is cooked through.
6. Serve immediately.

Nutrients Per Serving:

Calories	349
Omega-3s	235mg
Total Fat	5g
Saturated Fat	2g
Protein	25g
Total Carbohydrate	52g
Cholesterol	57mg
Sodium	203mg
Fiber	4g

Hearty Baked Italian Stew

This stew is perfect for winter — a delicious, hot comfort food.

Prep Time	Cook Time	Yields
15-20 minutes	40-45 minutes	6 servings

1 lb.	catfish, or other white-fleshed fish, cut into 1-inch pieces
1 T.	olive oil
2	celery stalks, sliced
1½ C.	carrots, sliced
7 C.	boiling water
1 C.	onion, chopped
1	garlic clove, minced
1	14.5 oz. can crushed tomatoes, undrained
2	cubes chicken bouillon
½ C.	lentils, rinsed
½ C.	pearl barley
1 tsp.	Italian seasoning or dried oregano
1 tsp.	dried basil, crushed
1 tsp.	dried rosemary, crushed
¼ tsp.	ground pepper

1. Preheat oven to 375°F.
2. Add all ingredients except fish to an oven-proof dish.
3. Cover. Bake for 30 minutes.
4. Add fish. Cover. Bake for 10 minutes.
5. Do not stir. It will break up fish.

Substitutions: scallops, shrimp, squid

Nutrients Per Serving:

Calories	285
Omega-3s	316mg
Total Fat	9g
Saturated Fat	3g
Protein	20g
Total Carbohydrate	34g
Cholesterol	41mg
Sodium	570mg
Fiber	10g

Italian Cioppino

This is a wonderful versatile recipe. Add more vegetables such as carrots and zucchini and serve it over rice or pasta.

Prep Time	Cook Time	Yields
15-20 minutes	40 minutes	6 servings

1½ lbs.	cod, boneless, skinless, cut in ½-inch cubes
1 T.	olive oil
1 C.	onion, chopped
2	garlic cloves, minced
1 T.	olive oil
1	8 oz. can tomato sauce
1	28 oz. can diced tomatoes, undrained
½ C.	dry white wine, or water
1 tsp.	each dried basil, thyme, marjoram, oregano
1 tsp.	sugar
1	bay leaf
¼ tsp.	black pepper
4	whole cloves (optional)
1 T.	fresh parsley, minced, to garnish

1. Heat olive oil in a 4-quart saucepan, sauté onion and garlic until tender.
2. Add tomato sauce, tomatoes, wine/water and all seasonings except parsley.
3. Simmer covered for 20 minutes, stirring occasionally.
4. Add fish and cook about 10 minutes.
5. Remove bay leaf and cloves before serving.
6. Garnish with parsley.

Substitutions: haddock, shrimp, perch

Nutrients Per Serving:

Calories	186
Omega-3s	244mg
Total Fat	4g
Saturated Fat	1g
Protein	23g
Total Carbohydrate	17g
Cholesterol	49mg
Sodium	244mg
Fiber	4g

Louisiana Gumbo

Prep Time	Cook Time	Yields
15-20 minutes	75 minutes	8 servings

1½ lb.	raw shrimp, peeled, deveined
1 T.	butter
1 T.	flour
1	onion, finely chopped
1 C.	ham, finely chopped
1	10 oz. package frozen okra, thawed, chopped
2¼ C.	fish stock or water
3	stalks celery, sliced
1	14.5 oz. can tomatoes, undrained
2 T.	fresh parsley, chopped
1	green bell pepper, chopped
1 tsp.	salt
½ tsp.	pepper
1	garlic clove, minced
¼ tsp.	dried thyme
¼ tsp.	dried oregano
2	bay leaves

Tip: For authentic gumbo, after peeling shrimp and before starting gumbo, boil shrimp shells and 2½ C. water for 10 minutes. Strain. Use in gumbo recipe for fish stock.

1. Melt butter and whisk in flour in heavy 4-quart saucepan over medium heat, cooking until golden brown, about 5 minutes.
2. Add onion and sauté until transparent.
3. Reduce heat. Add ham, okra. Cook for 10 minutes, stirring constantly.
4. Add fish stock, celery, tomatoes, parsley, green pepper, salt, pepper and spices. Reduce heat, cover, simmer for 45 minutes.
5. Add shrimp, cook for 15 minutes.
6. Serve over brown rice.

Substitutions: crawfish, clam meat

Nutrients Per Serving:

Calories	163
Omega-3s	294mg
Total Fat	4g
Saturated Fat	1g
Protein	23g
Total Carbohydrate	11g
Cholesterol	176mg
Sodium	778mg
Fiber	3g

Mediterranean Fish Stew

Prep Time	Cook Time	Yields
10-15 minutes	30-35 minutes	6 servings

1½ lbs. bass, cut into 1-inch cubes
2   carrots, sliced
2   stalks celery, sliced
½ C.   onion, chopped
2   garlic cloves, minced
2 T.   olive oil
1   28 oz. can tomatoes, undrained
1 C.   water
3 T.   fresh parsley, minced, or 1 T. dried parsley
1 cube chicken bouillon
½ tsp. dried oregano
¼ tsp. dried thyme
¼ tsp. dried basil
⅛ tsp. pepper

1. Heat oil in a 4-quart saucepan; sauté carrots, celery, onion, garlic for 5 minutes.
2. Add undrained tomatoes, water, 2 T. fresh parsley, bouillon, spices.
3. Cover and simmer for 20 minutes.
4. Add fish to stew. Cover and simmer for 5-10 minutes.
5. Sprinkle with remaining parsley.
6. Serve over whole-wheat pasta or rice.

Substitutions: cod, tilapia, squid

Nutrients Per Serving:

Calories	196
Omega-3s	233mg
Total Fat	6g
Saturated Fat	1g
Protein	23g
Total Carbohydrate	14g
Cholesterol	49mg
Sodium	455mg
Fiber	4g

Mexican Pescado Soup

Prep Time	Cook Time	Yields
5-10 minutes	25-30 minutes	4 servings

1 lb.	white-fleshed fish, such as cod or grouper cut into 2-inch pieces
6 C.	reduced-sodium chicken stock
⅔ C.	rice
2 C.	corn kernels, frozen
2 C.	chunky salsa

Lime wedges, to garnish

1. Combine stock and rice in a 3-quart pan.
2. Bring to a boil. Turn heat down. Cover, simmer for 15-20 minutes or until rice is tender.
3. Add fish, corn, salsa.
4. Cover and simmer about 10 minutes.
5. Serve with lime wedges.

Substitutions: crab legs, clams, mussels, crawfish in shell

Nutrients Per Serving:

Calories	213
Omega-3s	250 mg
Total Fat	4g
Saturated Fat	0g
Protein	29g
Total Carbohydrate	74g
Cholesterol	55mg
Sodium	618mg
Fiber	3g

Holiday Oyster Stew

On Christmas Eve our family would have oyster stew. The warm savory milk would lull us into sweet dreams anticipating Christmas day.

Prep Time	Cook Time	Yields
5-10 minutes	10-15 minutes	4 servings

1 pint   extra-small oysters, undrained
1 C.   water
½ C.   onion, finely chopped
¼ C.   fresh celery leaves, chopped
¼ tsp.   white pepper
2 C.   half and half cream
1 T.   Worcestershire sauce
3 drops Tabasco, or other hot sauce, to taste
dash   mace, optional

1. In a 3-quart saucepan, add oysters, water, onion, celery leaves, pepper.
2. Simmer for 5 minutes, covered, stirring occasionally.
3. Add cream, Worcestershire and Tabasco sauce. Slowly heat to steaming. Do not boil.
4. Serve immediately.

Substitutions: scallops, crab meat, lobster

Tip: *Oysters are priced by size. The smallest ones cost more but are worth the price!*

Nutrients Per Serving:

Calories	267
Omega-3s	427mg
Total Fat	5g
Saturated Fat	2g
Protein	13g
Total Carbohydrate	17g
Cholesterol	48mg
Sodium	290mg
Fiber	1g

Restaurant Style Salmon Bisque

Prep Time	Cook Time	Yields
15-20 minutes	15-20 minutes	4 servings

1	7 oz. can red salmon, undrained
1	15 oz. can sweet potatoes, drained
1	10.75 oz. can condensed tomato soup
½	sweet onion, minced
3	garlic cloves, minced
2 C.	chicken broth
1 tsp.	dried rosemary
1 tsp.	curry powder
½ tsp.	dried thyme
¼ tsp.	cayenne pepper
1 C.	low-fat milk

Tip: *To reduce sodium, use low sodium products.*

1. Simmer sweet potatoes, tomato soup, onion, garlic, chicken broth, spices in a 3-quart saucepan for 10 minutes.
2. Pour soup into a blender or food processor, add salmon, purée on high until completely smooth.
3. Pour soup back into saucepan. Place on stove.
4. Add milk and cook over medium heat, but do not boil.
5. Check consistency: if it is too thick, add a few tablespoons of milk; If it isn't thick enough, cook a little bit longer, being careful it doesn't boil.

Substitutions: yesterday's boneless and skinless grilled salmon

Nutrients Per Serving:

Calories	204
Omega-3s	566mg
Total Fat	6g
Saturated Fat	2g
Protein	11g
Total Carbohydrate	28g
Cholesterol	24mg
Sodium	889mg
Fiber	3g

Saturday Night Salmon-Potato Chowder

Chowder purists argue about precisely how the soup should be prepared—some insist on adding salt pork or bacon, others want no seasoning but salt and pepper. I have made hundreds of gallons of delicious chowder, soup, stew and broth using every recipe combination known to fishermen. Don't worry about the purists— just enjoy.

Prep Time	Cook Time	Yields
10-15 minutes	25-30 minutes	4 servings

2	7 oz. pouches salmon
1 tsp.	canola oil
3 T.	onion, chopped
3 T.	celery, chopped
1 C.	reduced-sodium chicken stock
⅔ C.	corn, frozen
⅔ C.	red potatoes, diced
¼ C.	water
¼ tsp.	dried thyme
⅛ tsp.	garlic powder
⅛ tsp.	ground white pepper
⅛ tsp.	salt
1 C.	evaporated low-fat milk

1. Heat oil in a 2-quart saucepan. Sauté onions and celery until translucent.
2. Add chicken stock, corn, potatoes, water, seasonings. Stir.
3. Cover and simmer, stirring occasionally, for 10-15 minutes, until potatoes are on the firm side of tender.
4. Add salmon and milk, stir, heat on low until thoroughly warm.
5. Serve with crackers.

Substitutions: salmon (boneless, skinless) cut into 2-inch cubes

Tip: *To thicken, add 2 T. flour slowly at step 2.*

Nutrients Per Serving:

Calories	224
Omega-3s	1,347mg
Total Fat	7g
Saturated Fat	2g
Protein	23g
Total Carbohydrate	18g
Cholesterol	45mg
Sodium	777mg
Fiber	1g

Seafood Chili

Prep Time	Cook Time	Yields
10-15 minutes	40 minutes	4 servings

1 lb.	scallops or shrimp meat
1	10 oz. can chicken stock
1	onion, finely chopped
1	garlic clove, minced
1 tsp.	dried oregano
1	15 oz. can lima beans, drained, rinsed
1	4 oz. can green chilies, diced
1	4 oz. can tomato sauce
3 T.	chili powder
1 T.	ground cumin
½ C.	water, or as needed
1 tsp.	cayenne pepper (optional)

Tip: *Serve with a pot of cooked brown rice. Top chili with chopped onions, black olives, or grated cheese.*

1. Mix chicken stock, onion, garlic, oregano in a 2-quart saucepan.
2. Cover and simmer over low heat for 15 minutes.
3. Add beans, chilies, tomato sauce, chili powder, cumin.
4. Cover and simmer for 20 minutes.
5. Add water until chili is the thickness you want. Taste to make sure it's spicy enough – if it isn't, add cayenne.
6. Add shrimp and cook over medium heat for 10 minutes.

Nutrients Per Serving:

Calories	272
Omega-3s	343mg
Total Fat	3g
Saturated Fat	1g
Protein	29g
Total Carbohydrate	34g
Cholesterol	37mg
Sodium	647mg
Fiber	8g

Holiday Shrimp Bisque

Prep Time	Cook Time	Yields
15-20 minutes	30-35 minutes	6 servings

1½ lb.	raw shrimp, shelled, deveined
1 T.	butter
¼ C.	onion, chopped
2 T.	celery, chopped
2 T.	carrot, chopped
4 C.	chicken broth
½ tsp.	dried thyme
1	bay leaf
2 T.	flour
¼ C.	dry sherry
½ tsp.	each, salt, white pepper
Dash	hot sauce
2 T.	heavy cream
1 T.	parsley, chopped

1. Melt butter in a 3-quart saucepan. Sweat onion, celery, carrot for 10 minutes.
2. Add chicken broth, shrimp, thyme, bay leaf. Bring to a boil. Reduce heat. Simmer for 10 minutes.
3. Pour shrimp and vegetables through a strainer. Reserve all stock in a bowl.
4. Remove bay leaf. Put strained shrimp and vegetables and 1 C. reserved stock in a blender or food processor. Puree at high speed until smooth. Pour into saucepan.
5. Mix ½ C. of reserved stock with flour and set aside.
6. Blend shrimp puree, flour/stock mixture, sherry. Bring to a boil. Reduce heat.
7. Stir in heavy cream. Add salt, pepper and hot sauce to taste. Heat until bisque is very hot. Do not boil.
8. Garnish with parsley.

Tip: *To sweat vegetables means to cook on low heat, covered. It pulls the moisture out and intensifies the flavors of the vegetables.*

Nutrients Per Serving:

Calories	324
Omega-3s	294mg
Total Fat	5g
Saturated Fat	2g
Protein	23g
Total Carbohydrate	11g
Cholesterol	176mg
Sodium	541mg
Fiber	3g

Thai Shrimp Soup

Wonderful! Distinctive herbs from Asia will make a big difference in flavor.

Prep Time	Cook Time	Yields
15-20 minutes	35 minutes	6 servings

½ lb.	raw shrimp, peeled, deveined
¼ lb.	catfish, cut into bite-sized pieces
1	chicken breast, skinless, cut into bite-sized pieces
1 C.	carrots, cut into chunks
1 C.	celery, thickly sliced
1 C.	sweet potato, peeled, cut into chunks
1 C.	onion, chopped
2	garlic cloves, minced
4 C.	water
2 cubes	chicken bouillon
1	14 oz. can low-fat coconut milk
½ tsp.	crushed red pepper flakes
1 tsp.	turmeric
1 tsp.	curry powder
1 tsp.	galangal (ginger), grated
½ C.	fresh Thai basil, chopped
½ C.	cilantro, chopped

Tip: *Thicken with 2 T. corn starch slurry.*

1. Stir chicken, carrots, celery, sweet potato, onion, garlic, water and bouillon in a 3-quart saucepan. Simmer for 20 minutes. Stir occasionally.
2. Add coconut milk, seasonings, slurry (if desired), catfish. Simmer for 10 minutes.
3. Add shrimp, cook for 5 minutes.
4. Garnish with basil and cilantro.

Substitutions: snapper, salmon, scallops

Nutrients Per Serving:

Calories	199
Omega-3s	208mg
Total Fat	7g
Saturated Fat	5g
Protein	22g
Total Carbohydrate	11g
Cholesterol	105mg
Sodium	530mg
Fiber	3g

U.S. Army Seafood Stew

For several years I worked with the military to develop seafood recipes for troop meals. More seafood is being served to the troops for the nutritional benefits.

Prep Time	Cook Time	Yields
15-20 minutes	30-35 minutes	6 servings or 4 hungry soldiers

¾ lb.   cod, cut into bite-sized pieces
½ lb.   raw shrimp, peeled, deveined
1 T.   olive oil
¾ C.   green bell pepper, chopped
¾ C.   red bell pepper, chopped
⅓ C.   onion, chopped
1½ tsp. chili powder
1½ tsp. Old Bay seasoning
½ tsp.   garlic powder
⅔ C.   fresh orange juice
1¼ C.   chicken broth
1   14.5 oz. can crushed tomatoes, undrained
1½ C.   long grain rice

Tip: *To make your own fresh Old Bay seasoning, see the recipe on page 219 in the Sauces, Marinades, Salsas, Rubs chapter.*

1. Preheat a 3-quart saucepan on medium heat. Add oil.
2. Cook peppers and onions in saucepan for 5 minutes, stirring constantly.
3. Add chili powder, Old Bay seasoning, garlic powder, stir.
4. Pour in orange juice, chicken broth, tomatoes, rice. Bring to a boil.
5. Cover, reduce heat to low, simmer for 20 minutes or until rice is tender.
6. Add fish and simmer for 4 minutes. Add shrimp. Stir. Simmer 3 minutes.

Substitutions: canned or pouched salmon

Nutrients Per Serving:

Calories	313
Omega-3s	335mg
Total Fat	2g
Saturated Fat	0.5g
Protein	24g
Total Carbohydrate	49g
Cholesterol	82mg
Sodium	513mg
Fiber	3g

Chapter 7

Salads

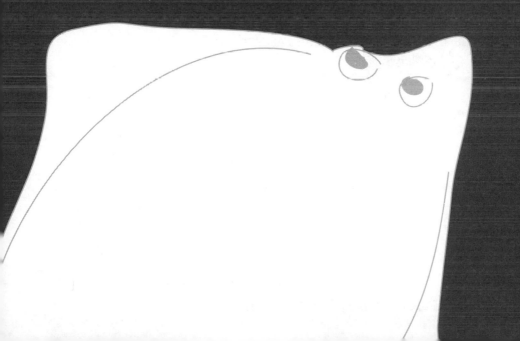

Amazingly Delicious Curry Tuna Salad with Fruit

This salad is a favorite standby for unexpected company or a lazy summer day.

Prep Time	Cook Time	Yields
5-10 minutes	None	4 servings

1	7 oz. can Albacore tuna in water, drained (save), flaked
1½ C.	fruit: grapes (halved), cantaloupe balls, or honeydew melon (cubed)
½ C.	celery, sliced
8	romaine lettuce leaves, shredded
¼ C.	toasted almonds, to garnish (optional)

Curry Dressing

2. T.	saved tuna liquid
2 T.	fresh lemon juice
1 T.	honey
1 T.	grated lemon zest
¼ tsp.	ground ginger
¼ tsp.	curry powder

1. Mix dressing in a medium sized bowl.
2. Add tuna, fruit, celery, lettuce. Toss lightly to coat.
3. Garnish with almonds, if desired.

Substitutions: canned salmon or leftover cooked seafood.

Nutrients Per Serving:

Calories	105
Omega-3s	415mg
Total Fat	1g
Saturated Fat	0g
Protein	11g
Total Carbohydrate	14g
Cholesterol	18mg
Sodium	172mg
Fiber	1g

Asian Shrimp and Rice Noodles

Prep Time	Cook Time	Yields
15-20 minutes	8-10 minutes	4 servings

1 lb.	cooked shrimp, peeled, deveined
6 C.	water
6 C.	rice noodles
2	green onions, thinly sliced
1	red bell pepper, cut in thin strips
1	English cucumber, cut in thin strips
1	carrot, peeled, cut in thin strips
4 C.	cabbage, shredded
½ C.	fresh cilantro, finely chopped
½ C.	walnuts, chopped

Dressing

½ C.	low-fat Ranch dressing
1 tsp.	ground ginger
1 tsp.	wasabi
½ tsp.	sesame oil

1. Bring water to a boil in a medium pot.
2. Add rice noodles and cook for 3-4 minutes. Rinse in cold water. Drain thoroughly. Return rinsed noodles to pot.
3. Add onion, pepper, cucumber, carrot to noodles. Gently mix.
4. Whisk dressing ingredients in a small bowl.
5. Divide cabbage onto four plates. Place noodles with vegetables over cabbage.
6. Sprinkle cilantro evenly over noodles.
7. Place cooked shrimp on top of noodle mixture.
8. Evenly drizzle dressing over salads and garnish with walnuts.

Substitutions: surimi, crab meat

Nutrients Per Serving:

Calories	410
Omega-3s	277mg
Total Fat	23g
Saturated Fat	3g
Protein	28g
Total Carbohydrate	25g
Cholesterol	221mg
Sodium	600mg
Fiber	4g

Blackened Salmon Caesar Salad

At *several outdoor events in the greater Seattle area, this salad is the most popular food, judging from the long line at the booth.*

Prep Time	Cook Time	Yields
15 minutes	10 minutes	4 servings

4- 4oz. salmon fillets, boneless, skinless
canola oil

Blackened Seasoning
2 T. paprika, ground
1 T. cayenne pepper, ground
1 T. onion powder
1 tsp. salt
½ tsp. white pepper
½ tsp. black pepper
¼ tsp. thyme, ground
¼ tsp. dried basil
¼ tsp. dried oregano

1 bunch romaine lettuce, chopped
Caesar salad dressing

1. Mix blackened seasoning in a jar with a tight lid.
2. Toss lettuce with Caesar salad dressing. Refrigerate.
3. Coat salmon with oil. Evenly sprinkle blackened seasoning on both sides of salmon.
4. Heat large skillet on high. Cook fillets 3 minutes, turn and continue cooking until fish is done.
5. Serve ¼ of Caesar salad on each plate. Top with blackened salmon.

Substitutions: tuna, tilapia, trout

Tip: *Store seasoning in a jar with a tight lid in a cool dry place.*

Nutrients Per Serving:

Calories	207
Omega-3s	823mg
Total Fat	6g
Saturated Fat	1g
Protein	22g
Total Carbohydrate	8g
Cholesterol	45mg
Sodium	403mg
Fiber	1g

Couscous Salmon Salad

Prep Time	Cook Time	Yields
5-10 minutes	about 10 minutes	4 servings

1 lb.	salmon, cooked, boneless, skinless
1 C.	chicken broth
½ tsp.	ground cumin
½ tsp.	turmeric
¼ tsp.	cayenne pepper
¼ tsp.	coriander
2 T.	rosemary
¾ C.	couscous, uncooked
1	garlic clove, minced
1 tsp.	olive oil
2	green onions, chopped
1	red bell pepper, diced

Fresh-ground black pepper to taste

1. Boil broth with spices in a 2-qt. saucepan.
2. Stir in couscous, cover. Remove from heat. Sit for 5 minutes.
3. Sauté garlic, green onion, bell pepper in an oiled frying pan for 2 minutes.
4. Add couscous to fry pan and gently stir salmon into couscous.

Substitutions: canned tuna, leftover cooked seafood

Nutrients Per Serving:

Calories	357
Omega-3s	145mg
Total Fat	12g
Saturated Fat	5g
Protein	22g
Total Carbohydrate	15g
Cholesterol	46mg
Sodium	310mg
Fiber	3g

Dijon Pasta Salad with Salmon

Alaska salmon processors used this recipe to promote their pouched salmon at supermarkets.

Prep Time	Cook Time	Yields
10-15 minutes	10-12 minutes	6 servings

2	7 oz. pouches of canned salmon, drained, flaked
11 oz.	petite sea shell pasta
2	Roma tomatoes, seeded, cut into eighths
2	green onions, chopped
1	cucumber, sliced

Dressing

½ C.	low-fat sour cream
½ C.	low-fat mayonnaise
2 T.	Dijon mustard
2 T.	fresh lemon juice
2 tsp.	dried dill
¾ tsp.	salt
¼ tsp.	pepper

Tip: *Can be prepared a day ahead. Cover. Refrigerate.*

1. Cook pasta according to directions on package.
2. Drain and cool.
3. Whisk dressing ingredients in a large serving bowl.
4. Add cooled pasta and vegetables. Toss to coat.
5. Gently fold in salmon.
6. Serve.

Substitutions: canned tuna, smoked salmon, leftover cooked fish

Nutrients Per Serving:

Calories	339
Omega-3s	744mg
Total Fat	8g
Saturated Fat	3g
Protein	20g
Total Carbohydrate	44g
Cholesterol	34mg
Sodium	485mg
Fiber	2g

Doug's Shrimp Pea Salad

This is a mandatory salad for our family gatherings. My brother, Doug, has to bring this dish because it is so delicious. It's wonderful with smoked salmon too!

Prep Time	Cook Time	Yields
20-25 minutes	0 minutes	6 servings

Salad
½ lb.	cooked salad shrimp
3	hard boiled eggs, chopped
1	16 oz. package frozen petite peas
¼ C.	red bell pepper, chopped
¼ C.	Gouda cheese, smoked, diced
2 T.	almonds, smoked, chopped

Dressing
½ C.	low-fat mayonnaise
½ C.	plain low-fat yogurt
½ C.	white sweet onion, chopped
½ tsp.	dried dill

The day before
1. Mix dressing. Cover. Refrigerate.
2. Boil eggs and refrigerate.

Day of
1. Thaw peas and shrimp if frozen, drain. Use a paper towel to dry peas and shrimp.
2. Shell and chop eggs.
3. Combine all ingredients in a medium serving bowl and gently toss.
4. Serve immediately.

Substitutions: smoked salmon

Nutrients Per Serving:

Calories	270
Omega-3s	204mg
Total Fat	14g
Saturated Fat	4g
Protein	19g
Total Carbohydrate	16g
Cholesterol	200mg
Sodium	430mg
Fiber	5g

Garden Fresh Tuna Salad

Prep Time	Cook Time	Yields
15-20 minutes	None	4 servings

2	6 oz. cans Albacore tuna, drained, flaked
4 C.	iceberg lettuce, shredded
2	green onions, finely chopped
½ C.	green bell pepper, diced
½ C.	cucumber, sliced
½ C.	frozen peas, defrosted
½ tsp.	garlic powder
½ C.	mozzarella cheese, grated
2	tomatoes, cut into wedges
2 T.	parsley, chopped

Dressing

1 C.	plain low-fat yogurt
2 T.	low-fat mayonnaise
½ tsp.	black pepper
½ tsp.	dried dill
½ tsp.	prepared horseradish

Tip: *Red peppers instead of green, for a color and flavor contrast.*

1. Mix all dressing ingredients in a small bowl.
2. Toss lettuce, green onion, pepper, cucumber, peas in a glass bowl.
3. Sprinkle with garlic powder and toss again.
4. Break apart chunks of tuna with a fork in a separate bowl. Place on top of greens.
5. Pour dressing over fish and garnish with cheese, tomato wedges, parsley.
6. Serve immediately.

Substitutions: cooked salmon, shrimp, surimi, poached fresh albacore tuna

Nutrients Per Serving:

Calories	223
Omega-3s	761mg
Total Fat	8g
Saturated Fat	3g
Protein	26g
Total Carbohydrate	12g
Cholesterol	45mg
Sodium	486mg
Fiber	3g

French Cut Green Bean Salmon Salad

Prep Time	Cook Time	Yields
20-25 minutes	20-25 minutes	4 Servings

1 lb.	salmon fillet, skinless, cut into 12 pieces
1 cup	French cut green beans, fresh or frozen
2 T.	honey
2 T.	fresh lemon juice
1/8 tsp.	black pepper
1/4 tsp.	salt

Dressing

1/4 C.	olive oil
2 T.	orange juice
2 T.	bacon bits
2 tsp.	Dijon mustard
2 tsp.	honey
1/4 tsp.	salt

4 C.	salad greens

Tip: *Steps 1 and 2 may be done ahead of time.*

1. Microwave green beans for about 3 minutes, until cooked through but not mushy. To shock, prepare a bowl of cold water enough to submerge beans. Shock beans to stop cooking and retain bright green color.
2. Drain thoroughly, pat dry, cool.
3. Mix honey, lemon juice, pepper in a small bowl; brush over salmon.
4. Cook salmon in a skillet over high heat for 3-5 minutes on each side, until cooked through. Season with salt.
5. Whisk dressing ingredients in a small bowl.
6. Toss beans with salad greens in large bowl. Divide onto 4 plates.
7. Place 3 salmon pieces on each plate. Serve with dressing.

Substitutions: tuna, scallops, trout

Nutrients Per Serving:

Calories	232
Omega-3s	645mg
Total Fat	5g
Saturated Fat	1g
Protein	20g
Total Carbohydrate	12g
Cholesterol	40mg
Sodium	90mg
Fiber	3g

Norwegian Herring Apple Salad

Prep Time	Cook Time	Yields
5-10 minutes	None	4 servings

1   16 oz. jar pickled herring, drained and cut into tidbit sized pieces
1   Granny Smith apple, peeled, cored, finely chopped
½ C.   red onion, finely chopped
½ tsp.   dried dill
¼ C.   low-fat sour cream
1 ½ tsp. Dijon mustard

1. Combine herring, apple, onion in a medium bowl.
2. Mix dill, sour cream and mustard in a small bowl. Add to herring mixture.
3. Stir, cover, refrigerate for several hours to blend flavors.
4. Serve with whole grain bread.

Substitutions: pickled salmon, or sardines; pear instead of apple

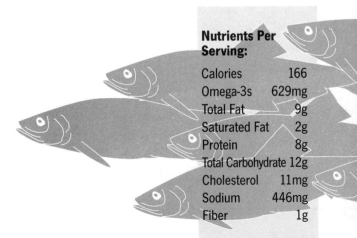

Nutrients Per Serving:

Calories	166
Omega-3s	629mg
Total Fat	9g
Saturated Fat	2g
Protein	8g
Total Carbohydrate	12g
Cholesterol	11mg
Sodium	446mg
Fiber	1g

Avocado and Shrimp Salad

Prep Time	Cook Time	Yields
15-20 minutes	None	6 servings

		Dressing	
½ lb.	surimi		
½ lb.	cooked salad shrimp	⅛ C.	cilantro, chopped
2	Roma tomatoes, seeded, diced	¼ C.	red onion, finely diced
1	orange, peeled, diced	2 T.	olive oil
		2 T.	fresh lime juice
1	poblano pepper, chopped	1 tsp.	kosher salt
			Pepper, to taste
1	avocado, diced		

1. Whisk dressing ingredients in a small bowl. Set aside.
2. Chop surimi (imitation crab) into bite-sized pieces.
3. Put chopped crab, shrimp, tomatoes, oranges and pepper into a medium-sized serving bowl.
4. Pour dressing onto salad.
5. Toss all ingredients, except for avocado, with dressing.
6. Add avocado (see below). Mix gently.
7. Serve immediately.

To dice an avocado
1. Cut avocado in half, rolling knife blade around seed.
2. Twist halves, one in each hand, to separate.
3. With a knife, carefully hit seed on top to slightly embed knife. Twist to loosen and lift seed out.
4. Hold one avocado half in one hand; with other hand, use knife tip to gently cut strips lengthwise into avocado. Do not cut all the way through avocado skin!
5. Cut across avocado, to make ¼-inch slices.
6. Take avocado by the edges and gently turn inside out. Beautifully diced avocado chunks should fall into your salad. Help them out with a spoon, if needed.
7. Repeat with other half.

Substitutions: crab or lobster meat

Nutrients Per Serving:

Calories	155
Omega-3s	451mg
Total Fat	6g
Saturated Fat	1g
Protein	12g
Total Carbohydrate	16g
Cholesterol	48mg
Sodium	915mg
Fiber	4g

Savory Slaw with Shrimp

This is a quick, easy meal for a hot summer night! It's easy for the kids to prepare, too.

Prep Time	Cook Time	Yields
5-10 minutes	None	4 servings

½ lb.   cooked salad shrimp
1   16 oz. bag coleslaw mix
2 T.   fresh cilantro, chopped

Dressing
½ C.   low-fat mayonnaise
2 T.   sugar
2 T.   fresh lime juice
¾ tsp.   salt
¼ tsp.   ground ginger

1. Mix dressing ingredients in a small bowl. Set aside.
2. Toss coleslaw and cilantro in a medium serving bowl.
3. Add dressing and shrimp to slaw mixture and gently toss.
4. Chill, if desired.

Substitutions: Canned tuna, salmon, surimi; fresh parsley in place of cilantro

Tip: *Tasty as a sandwich filling.*

Nutrients Per Serving:

Calories	210
Omega-3s	228mg
Total Fat	11g
Saturated Fat	2g
Protein	14g
Total Carbohydrate	15g
Cholesterol	121mg
Sodium	825mg
Fiber	3g

Shrimp Remoulade

This classic Creole appetizer is excellent as a salad or main dish.

Prep Time	Cook Time	Yields
10 minutes	None	6 servings

1 lb.　cooked shrimp, large, peeled
1 head　iceberg lettuce, thinly sliced into ribbons

Remoulade Sauce

1	celery stalk, chopped
½	sweet onion, chopped
¼	bunch parsley, chopped
1 C.	sun-dried tomatoes
2 T.	Dijon mustard
2 T.	red wine vinegar
1 T.	prepared horseradish sauce
2 tsp.	cayenne pepper
1 tsp	Worcestershire sauce
¼ C.	olive oil

Tip: *On a hot day make four generous dinner salads. Serve with fruit slices and chilled wine.*

1. Chop celery, onion, parsley in a food processor until finely minced.
2. Add remaining ingredients except olive oil. Process until well blended.
3. Drizzle olive oil slowly into sauce, continue mixing until smooth.
4. Refrigerate overnight.
5. Coat shrimp with sauce, toss gently.
6. Divide lettuce among 6 chilled salad plates. Divide shrimp evenly atop the lettuce.

Substitutions: poached scallops, surimi

Nutrients Per Serving:

Calories	212
Omega-3s	366mg
Total Fat	10g
Saturated Fat	2g
Protein	31g
Total Carbohydrate	11g
Cholesterol	173mg
Sodium	590mg
Fiber	3g

Crab and Pasta Salad

Crab is very sweet and goes well with fruit. Exchange fruit for vegetables in this recipe and it will take on a wonderful new flavor. Enjoy mangos, cantaloupe, bananas, pineapple, or strawberries.

Prep Time	Cook Time	Yields
15-20 minutes	10-12 minutes	4 servings

8 oz.	surimi
8 oz.	shell pasta, cooked
1 tsp.	each oregano, basil, parsley, mint; chopped
2 tsp.	olive oil
2	celery stalks, thinly sliced
½	sweet onion, chopped
½	red bell pepper, chopped
½ C.	low-fat sour cream

1. Cook pasta according to package. Drain, put into a large serving bowl, sprinkle herbs over pasta. Toss immediately with olive oil. Cool.
2. Stir vegetables into pasta; mix with sour cream.
3. Gently fold in surimi.
4. Serve chilled.

Substitutions: cooked lobster, salmon, tuna

Tip: *Can be made the day before, covered and refrigerated until serving.*

Nutrients Per Serving:

Calories	328
Omega-3s	411mg
Total Fat	4g
Saturated Fat	1g
Protein	16g
Total Carbohydrate	57g
Cholesterol	14mg
Sodium	543mg
Fiber	2g

Tuscan White Bean Salad with Tuna

Prep Time	Cook Time	Yields
20-25 minutes	None	4 servings

1	6 oz. can Albacore tuna, drained, flaked
1	15 oz. can white northern beans, drained
1	English cucumber, thinly sliced
1 bag	(4 C.) spinach leaves, washed
¾ C.	Italian parsley, coarsely chopped
2 T.	shallots, finely sliced
2 T.	kalamata olives, sliced

Dressing

3 T.	olive oil
1 tsp.	fresh lemon juice
¼ tsp.	each kosher salt, black pepper, oregano

1. Mix salad dressing in a small jar.
2. Mix tuna, beans and dressing in a medium sized serving bowl.
3. Toss spinach, cucumber, parsley, shallots and olives into mixture. Stir well.
4. Serve immediately.

Substitutions: Canned or smoked salmon, canned black beans, or kidney beans

Nutrients Per Serving:

Calories	282
Omega-3s	451mg
Total Fat	12g
Saturated Fat	2g
Protein	16g
Total Carbohydrate	29g
Cholesterol	12mg
Sodium	327mg
Fiber	7g

Chapter 8

Sandwiches

Albacore Tuna Sandwich

Albacore tuna is loaded with omega-3s. The tastiest tuna is canned in olive oil.

Prep Time	Cook Time	Yields
5-10 minutes	2 minutes	2 servings

1	7 oz. can Albacore tuna, drained, flaked
4	slices, whole-grain bread
2 tsp.	low-fat mayonnaise, or to taste
1 tsp.	lemon juice
Dash	black or white pepper

1. Toast bread.
2. Mix tuna, mayonnaise, pepper, lemon juice in a medium bowl.
3. Spread on toast.
4. Add any optional ingredients.
5. Cover with other slice of toast.
6. Slice in half.

Variations (mix into the tuna salad)

1 T.	pickle relish
1 T.	celery, finely chopped
1 T.	red bell pepper, chopped
2 tsp.	parsley, chopped
shake	garlic powder
shake	cayenne pepper
dash	Tabasco
dash	Worcestershire sauce

To the sandwiches

1	tomato, sliced
1	red onion, thinly sliced
1 C.	lettuce, shredded
1	cucumber, thinly sliced
2 slices	cheddar cheese
1 oz.	potato chips, baked

Tip: *Make this a bi-weekly brown-bagger!*

Nutrients Per Serving:

Calories	291
Omega-3s	832mg
Total Fat	6g
Saturated Fat	1g
Protein	25g
Total Carbohydrate	31g
Cholesterol	37mg
Sodium	783mg
Fiber	4g

Catfish Hoagie Sandwich

Pre-plan and cook extra seafood to make a delicious lunch sandwich tasty with left-over cole slaw.

Prep Time	Cook Time	Yields
5-10 minutes	8-10 minutes	1 serving

3 oz.   catfish fillet, (left-over)
2   slices bread (hoagie roll, 12 grain, ciabatta)
½ tsp. light mayonnaise
½ tsp. mustard
½ C.   cole slaw, left-over
1   small tomato, sliced

1. Toast bread.
2. Spread bread with mayonnaise and mustard.
3. Place fish on the mayonnaise coated slice.
4. Lay cole slaw and a tomato slice on fish.

Tip: *Drain cole slaw if it has gotten too soupy.*

Substitutions: grilled salmon, oysters, scallops

Nutrients Per Serving:

Calories	386
Omega-3s	326mg
Total Fat	12g
Saturated Fat	5g
Protein	32g
Total Carbohydrate	38g
Cholesterol	44mg
Sodium	739mg
Fiber	6g

Broiled Tuna Club Sandwich with Dill Mayonnaise

Prep Time	Cook Time	Yields
10 minutes	7 minutes	4 servings

4	4 oz. tuna fillets, boneless, skinless
12	bread slices, toasted
4	tomato slices
4	Canadian bacon slices
8	lettuce leaves

Herb Mayonnaise

¼ C.	low-fat mayonnaise
2 tsp.	dill, finely minced
1 tsp	dijon mustard

1. Mix mayonnaise, mustard, dill in a small bowl.
2. Toast bread.
3. Broil tuna.
4. Spread dill mayonnaise on both sides of four slices of bread.
5. Layer each sandwich in this order: 1 slice bread, 1 tuna fillet, 1 lettuce leaf, 1 slice dill/mayonnaise spread bread, 1 lettuce leaf, 1 tomato slice, 1 bacon slice, 1 slice bread.
6. Secure sandwich with sandwich picks, cut the sandwich into quarters. Serve.

Substitutions: salmon fillet or patty, pollock, sole

Tips: Add broiled eggplant and onions drizzled with olive oil. Organize the sandwich fixin's so assembly moves in a direct line.

Nutrients Per Serving:

Calories	467
Omega-3s	245mg
Total Fat	12g
Saturated Fat	7g
Protein	26g
Total Carbohydrate	42g
Cholesterol	65mg
Sodium	434mg
Fiber	3g

Grilled Salmon & Cheese

Prep Time	Cook Time	Yields
5 minutes	5 minutes	2 servings

4 oz.	smoked salmon, sliced
4	slices whole-wheat bread
2 oz.	pepper or colby jack cheese
2 tsp.	olive oil

1. Heat olive oil in a large frying pan on medium-high.
2. Make a sandwich by laying salmon and cheese between slices of bread.
3. Place sandwiches in pan.
4. Fry over medium heat until cheese melts and bread is toasty.
5. Cut in half and serve.

Substitutions: lox, smoked trout, whitefish

Nutrients Per Serving:

Calories	332
Omega-3s	388mg
Total Fat	17g
Saturated Fat	9g
Protein	22g
Total Carbohydrate	24g
Cholesterol	50mg
Sodium	1611mg
Fiber	4g

Salmon Pita Pocket

Use hummus as a low-fat sandwich spread, replacing mayonnaise.

Prep Time	Cook Time	Yields
5 minutes	None	1 serving

3 oz.	salmon (leftovers, canned or pouched)
1 half	whole wheat pita
1 T.	hummus, or mayonnaise
1 oz.	Mozzarella, sliced or feta cheese, crumbled
¾ C.	romaine lettuce, shredded
1	medium tomato, sliced
1 T.	low-fat sour cream, optional

1. Cut pita bread in half.
2. Open one half of pita and spread bottom with hummus.
3. Add cooked salmon.
4. Top that with cheese, lettuce, tomato.
5. Add a spoon of sour cream, if you like.

Hummus

1	15 oz. can chickpeas, rinsed, drained.
4	garlic cloves, minced
¼ C.	lemon juice
¼ C.	tahini (sesame paste)
1 T.	soy sauce

ground cayenne pepper and hot sauce to taste

1. Purée all ingredients in a food processor.
2. Spread on pita.
3. Enjoy as a dip with fresh cut vegetables.

Tip: *Chickpeas are also labeled garbanzo or ceci beans.*

Nutrients Per Serving:

Calories	406
Omega-3s	1,681mg
Total Fat	18g
Saturated Fat	6g
Protein	34g
Total Carbohydrate	27g
Cholesterol	90mg
Sodium	431mg
Fiber	4g

Salmon Salad Sandwiches

Processing seafood by canning, freezing, smoking or pickling does not change the Omega-3 content.

Prep Time	Cook Time	Yields
5-10 minutes	None	4 servings

1	7 oz. pouch or can of salmon, drained, flaked
1	hard boiled egg, chopped
½ C.	celery, chopped
¼ C.	low-fat mayonnaise
1 tsp.	onion, grated
Pinch	garlic powder
8	whole wheat bread slices
2 C.	romaine lettuce, shredded

Tip: *Toast bread before topping for a crispier sandwich.*

1. Mix salmon, egg, celery, mayonnaise, onion, garlic in a medium bowl.
2. Refrigerate, covered, for at least 10 minutes for flavors to blend.
3. Spread equally on four slices of bread, add lettuce, top with remaining slices of bread.
4. Cut each sandwich in half to serve.

Substitutions: other canned fish or leftover cooked fish; add an equal amount of chopped apple in place of the celery; add an equal proportion of Dijon mustard instead of the mayo.

Nutrients Per Serving:

Calories	310
Omega-3s	1,514mg
Total Fat	13g
Saturated Fat	3g
Protein	23g
Total Carbohydrate	26g
Cholesterol	80mg
Sodium	870mg
Fiber	4g

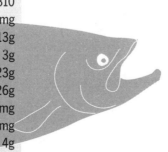

Smoked Salmon and Egg Muffin

Start adding essential Omega-3s to your breakfast meals.

Prep Time	Cook Time	Yields
5 minutes	5 minutes	1 serving

1 oz.	smoked salmon, sliced or crumbled
1 tsp.	low-fat cream cheese, spreadable
1	English muffin
1	egg, beaten
2 tsp.	milk
Dash	salt and pepper

1. Split and toast English muffin. Spread with cream cheese.
2. Mix egg, milk, salt and pepper in a small microwave proof bowl.
3. Microwave egg mixture on high for 1 minute.
4. Place salmon on one half of English muffin.
5. Arrange egg scramble on salmon, then top with other half of muffin.

Substitutions: kippers, smoked trout, whitefish

Tips: *Add 1 tsp. green chilies to egg scramble. Place one cheese and tomato slice on top of salmon.*

Nutrients Per Serving:

Calories	270
Omega-3s	217mg
Total Fat	8g
Saturated Fat	2g
Protein	18g
Total Carbohydrate	32g
Cholesterol	220mg
Sodium	1150mg
Fiber	2g

Garden Fresh Salmon Wrap

When I was introducing salmon into schools nationwide, a wrap became a lunchtime favorite.

Prep Time	Cook Time	Yields
15-20 minutes	None	4 servings

1	7 oz. can or pouch salmon, drained, flaked
2 tsp.	low-fat mayonnaise
2 T.	low-fat cream cheese, softened
2 drops	liquid smoke flavoring
⅛ tsp.	salt and pepper
¼ C.	carrots, shredded
¼ C.	celery, finely chopped
¼ C.	red bell pepper, finely chopped
4	12" whole wheat tortillas
1 C.	cheddar cheese, grated
2 C.	lettuce, shredded

1. Mix salmon, mayonnaise, cream cheese, liquid smoke, salt, pepper, in a bowl until smooth.
2. Spread salmon mixture evenly among four tortillas.
3. Sprinkle ¼ of vegetables over salmon.
4. Fold bottom of tortillas up, roll firmly from one side.

Substitutions: cooked shrimp, crab, tuna

Nutrients Per Serving:

Calories	410
Omega-3s	898mg
Total Fat	17g
Saturated Fat	7g
Protein	20g
Total Carbohydrate	44g
Cholesterol	50mg
Sodium	830mg
Fiber	4g

Fresh Salmon Burgers

Prep Time	Cook Time	Yields
5-10 minutes	8-10 minutes	4 servings

1 lb.	salmon, boneless, skinless
½ C.	bread crumbs
1 T.	Dijon mustard
1 T.	low-fat mayonnaise
1 T.	green onion, chopped
1 T.	low-sodium soy sauce
1 tsp.	prepared horseradish
1	egg, beaten
¼ tsp.	ground pepper
4	whole wheat buns
4	tomato slices
4	pineapple slices
4	lettuce leaves

1. Cut salmon into small pieces. Continue chopping until the salmon is finely minced.
2. Mix salmon, bread crumbs, mustard, mayonnaise, onion, soy sauce, horseradish, egg, ground pepper into a bowl. Stir.
3. Form into 4 patties. Cover. Chill.
4. Preheat oiled, foil lined broiler.
5. Place patties in broiler pan and cook 3 minutes. Turn.
6. Continue broiling until internal temperature reaches 145° F.
7. Place cooked burgers in bun and garnish.

Substitutions: tuna, white-fleshed fish

Nutrients Per Serving:

Calories	346
Omega-3s	1200mg
Total Fat	18g
Saturated Fat	3g
Protein	20g
Total Carbohydrate	4g
Cholesterol	60g
Sodium	327g
Fiber	1g

Chapter 9

Pasta, Noodles and Rice

Aromatic Seafood Rice

Prep Time	Cook Time	Yields
10-15 minutes	25-30 minutes	4 servings

1 lb.	cod, cut into 1-inch pieces
8 oz.	raw shrimp, peeled, deveined
1 T.	olive oil
1	onion, chopped
1	garlic clove, minced
2 tsp.	curry powder
1 tsp.	ground cumin
½ tsp.	chili powder
¼ tsp.	salt
¼ tsp.	pepper
¼ tsp.	cinnamon
¼ tsp.	ground cloves
1¼ C.	brown rice
2½ C.	boiling water
1 C.	frozen peas, thawed
1 C.	frozen corn kernels, thawed
1 T.	fresh lime juice

1. Heat olive oil on medium-high in a 3-quart pot.
2. Add onion, garlic and spices, stir for 1 minute.
3. Stir in rice, mixing until well coated with oil and spices.
4. Pour boiling water into saucepan.
5. Cover, turn heat to low (or warm) and simmer for 10 minutes.
6. Add fish, shrimp, peas, corn. Stir thoroughly.
7. Cover and cook for an additional 8 minutes, or until fish is cooked and rice is tender.
8. Fluff rice with a fork and sprinkle with lime juice.

Substitutions: mussels, crab, clams in shell

Nutrients Per Serving:

Calories	295
Omega-3s	367mg
Total Fat	4g
Saturated Fat	1g
Protein	25g
Total Carbohydrate	38g
Cholesterol	90mg
Sodium	231mg
Fiber	2g

Cannelloni with Crab and Shrimp

Prep Time	Cook Time	Yields
15 minutes	25-30 minutes	6 servings

¾ lb.   crab meat, cooked
¾ lb.   shrimp, cooked, peeled, deveined, chopped
½   red bell pepper, chopped
1   garlic clove, chopped
2 T.   olive oil
¼ C.   Romano cheese, grated
1 T.   parsley, chopped
1 tsp.   white wine, Chardonnay
¼ tsp.   black pepper
6 sheets cannelloni pasta (3" x 2¼" each)
1 C.   pesto

Tip: *To ease preparation, buy pesto instead of making it fresh, even though fresh is more flavorful. See recipe for fresh pesto on page 226.*

1. Purée bell pepper, garlic and olive oil in a blender or food processor. Transfer contents to a medium bowl. Gently blend with crab, shrimp, cheese, parsley, wine, pepper. Set aside.
2. Boil cannelloni in 3-quarts of water for about 9 minutes, or until soft.
3. Drain and gently lay each sheet side by side on clean, flat surface.
4. Pre-heat oven to 350° F.
5. Spread seafood mixture in a strip down each cannelloni, dividing evenly among sheets.
6. Roll each up and place them, side by side, in oiled baking dish.
7. Bake for 25 minutes at 350°F.
8. Slowly heat pesto. Spoon pesto over cannelloni.

Nutrients Per Serving:

Calories	346
Omega-3s	735mg
Total Fat	11g
Saturated Fat	3g
Protein	37g
Total Carbohydrate	22g
Cholesterol	194mg
Sodium	920mg
Fiber	3g

Dazzling Potluck Paella

Traveling in Spain taught me a love of paella. It is a big seafood eating country and paella is an open canvas for the catch of the day. Spanish recipes call for saffron which is a costly seasoning. I use turmeric which is tasty and less expensive.

Prep Time	Cook Time	Yields
20 minutes	30 minutes total	8 servings

1 lb.	uncooked shrimp, peeled, deveined
½ lb.	chicken, boneless, cut into ½- inch chunks
½ lb.	low-fat turkey sausage, diced
2 T.	olive oil
1	sweet onion, diced
1	red bell pepper, diced
2	carrots, diced
1 C.	sundried tomatoes, diced
2 T.	garlic, minced
6 C.	chicken broth, hot
1 C.	prepared salsa
3 C.	short or medium grain rice
1 C.	frozen peas
2 tsp.	turmeric
1 tsp.	Spanish smoked paprika, hot
2 T.	parsley, chopped

Tip: *Do not stir rice during cooking time which disturbs the socarrat, the crusty caramelized layer of rice on the bottom of pan.*

1. Heat oil in a large flat bottom skillet or paella pan until hot; add shrimp, chicken, sausage, onion, pepper, carrot, tomatoes and garlic to skillet. Brown for 10 minutes.
2. Pour in hot chicken broth, salsa, rice and return mixture to a boil. Add peas, turmeric and paprika to rice mixture. Stir to blend seasonings. Reduce heat to medium. Cook, uncovered for 10 minutes. Reduce heat to low and cook 8 more minutes.
3. Garnish with parsley.

Substitution: Squid, clams and mussels, in shell, king crab or jumbo shrimp, crawfish, lobster tails. Discard unopened clams or mussels before serving.

Nutrients Per Serving:

Calories	491
Omega-3s	246mg
Total Fat	14g
Saturated Fat	4g
Protein	40g
Total Carbohydrate	49g
Cholesterol	128mg
Sodium	966mg
Fiber	2g

Indonesian Fried Rice

Prep Time	Cook Time	Yields
15-20 minutes	10-15 minutes	4 servings

½ lb.   cooked shrimp, peeled, deveined
2   eggs, beaten
2 tsp.   sesame oil
½ tsp.   salt
1 T.   vegetable oil
3   green onions, thinly sliced
2   garlic cloves, minced
2 T.   ginger root, peeled and minced
3 C.   cooked rice (preferably day-old)
1 T.   fresh cilantro, chopped, to garnish (optional)

Tip: Use soy sauce for additional flavor.

1. Beat eggs, sesame oil and salt in a small bowl.
2. Heat oil in a large frying pan. Add green onions, garlic, ginger to pan and stir-fry for about 3 minutes.
3. Add eggs in a thin layer to pan and scramble over medium-low heat until done.
4. Stir in rice and shrimp. Mix until heated through.
5. Sprinkle with cilantro and serve.

Optional addition
½ C.   mushrooms, sliced
1   7 oz. can water chestnuts, drained, sliced
¼ C.   red bell pepper, finely diced

Nutrients Per Serving:

Calories	296
Omega-3s	260mg
Total Fat	9g
Saturated Fat	1g
Protein	16g
Total Carbohydrate	36g
Cholesterol	170mg
Sodium	845mg
Fiber	1g

Philippine Pansit and Shrimp

One summer I had fun working in an Alaskan salmon cannery. The workers came from all over the world to help in the harvest, bringing their traditional seafood recipes. Pansit was served at a birthday celebration.

Prep Time	Cook Time	Yields
15-20 minutes	20-25 minutes	6 servings

1 lb.	cooked shrimp, peeled, deveined
6 oz.	maifun (rice vermicelli)
1 T.	olive oil
1	onion, sliced
2 C.	frozen peas
1 C.	mushrooms, thinly sliced
1 C.	cabbage, thinly sliced
½ C.	carrots, grated
¼ C.	reduced-sodium soy sauce
1 C.	low-salt chicken broth

1. Soak maifun in hot water according to package directions, until soft, about 10 minutes.
2. Drain and cut into shorter lengths; set aside.
3. Heat frying pan on medium-high. Add oil and fry onions until soft. Add peas, mushroom, cabbage, carrots, soy sauce. Fry for 2 more minutes, stirring constantly.
4. Stir in chicken broth and bring to a full boil.
5. Lower heat, add shrimp, maifun and cook until liquid is gone.

Substitutions: cooked lobster, crab, clam meat

Tip: *Rice noodles, such as Maifun, can be found in the Asian section in most grocery stores. They are great for those who need to watch their gluten intake.*

Nutrients Per Serving:

Calories	220
Omega-3s	205mg
Total Fat	1g
Saturated Fat	1g
Protein	13g
Total Carbohydrate	39g
Cholesterol	57mg
Sodium	600mg
Fiber	5g

Quick Tomato-Tuna Sea Shells

The Mediterranean countries can their tuna in olive oil. It's a treat. If you can't find it, just add a few drops to the drained water packed albacore. It will liven it up.

Prep Time	Cook Time	Yields
15 minutes	15 minutes	4 servings

2	7 oz. cans albacore tuna, drained, flaked

Penne Sauce

1 tsp.	olive oil
1	garlic clove, minced
1	28 oz. can tomatoes, diced, undrained
2 T.	jalapeños, chopped
1 tsp.	dried basil, crumbled
½ tsp.	dried oregano, crushed
¼ tsp.	dried rosemary, crushed

Salt and pepper, to taste

2 C.	seashell pasta, or other type that holds sauce well
½ C.	mozzarella, shredded

1. Heat oil in a 2-quart pot; add sauce ingredients and simmer for 15 minutes.
2. Cook pasta according to directions on package, drain. Mix with sauce.
3. Gently stir tuna in sauce
4. Serve sprinkled with mozzarella.

Substitutions: leftover white fish from dinner the night before.

Tip: *Keep these ingredients on hand in the cupboard for a quick delicious meal.*

The brand of canned tomatoes will make a big taste difference. Use Sugo di Pomodoro, marinara or Al Dente! pasta sauce brands. They only can fresh, vine ripened tomatoes.

Nutrients Per Serving:

Calories	344
Omega-3s	281mg
Total Fat	5g
Saturated Fat	2g
Protein	32g
Total Carbohydrate	44g
Cholesterol	32mg
Sodium	695mg
Fiber	5g

Salmon Rigatoni

Fishermen from coast to coast have a similar combination of these ingredients and use the catch of the day. For instance, the sauce may be salsa, vegetables, green beans, asparagus, onions and the fish, grouper, halibut or lobster meat.

Prep Time	Cook Time	Yields
10 minutes	45 minutes	6 servings

1 lb.	salmon fillet, boneless and skinless, cut into 1-inch chunks
8 oz.	rigatoni pasta
1	26-oz. jar Classico Tomato & Basil sauce
¾ C.	red wine
¼ C.	lemon juice
½ lb.	mushrooms, cut into chunks
½ lb.	broccoli crowns
½ tsp.	black pepper
½ tsp.	garlic salt
½ tsp.	paprika
¼ lb.	sharp cheese, grated

Tip: *Al dente means to be cooked, but still firm.*

1. Preheat oven to 350° F.
2. Cook rigatoni very al dente. Drain. Place in single layer in an oiled 9 x13 baking pan.
3. Mix tomato sauce, wine, lemon juice in a bowl. Set aside.
4. Lay mushrooms, broccoli and salmon over rigatoni. Sprinkle with pepper and garlic salt.
5. Pour sauce evenly over pasta, vegetables and salmon.
6. Sprinkle with paprika. Top with cheese.
7. Bake, covered for 45 minutes.

Nutrients Per Serving:

Calories	279
Omega-3s	817mg
Total Fat	9g
Saturated Fat	3g
Protein	22g
Total Carbohydrate	33g
Cholesterol	148mg
Sodium	548 mg
Fiber	3g

Shrimp and Rice Pilaf

Prep Time	Cook Time	Yields
10-15 minutes	20-25 minutes	4 servings

1 lb.	cooked shrimp, peeled, deveined
¾ C.	jasmine rice, uncooked
1½ C.	water
1 T.	butter
3 T.	onion, chopped
2½ C.	tomatoes, chopped
3	celery stalks, chopped, save celery leaves
1	bay leaf
½ tsp.	brown sugar
¼ tsp.	salt
¼ tsp.	paprika
¼ C.	Parmesan cheese, grated (optional)

1. Simmer rice in a small covered pot for 15 minutes.
2. Melt butter in a 2-quart saucepan. Add onion, tomato, celery and leaves, seasoning. Simmer 10 minutes.
3. Remove celery leaves. Gently stir in shrimp until well-mixed.
4. Top with grated cheese, if you'd like.

Substitutions: Blend brown or wild rice in place of the jasmine rice for added color and nutrition.

Nutrients Per Serving:

Calories	232
Omega-3s	297mg
Total Fat	5g
Saturated Fat	2g
Protein	15g
Total Carbohydrate	33g
Cholesterol	94mg
Sodium	287mg
Fiber	2g

Singapore Shrimp Rice Noodles

Prep Time	Cook Time	Yields
20-25 minutes	15-20 minutes	4 servings

1 lb.   cooked medium shrimp, peeled, deveined
3 oz.   rice noodles (such as rice vermicelli)
2 tsp.   vegetable oil
1 T.   fresh ginger root, minced
1   garlic clove, minced
1   celery stalk, sliced
½   green bell pepper, seeded, chopped
½   sweet onion, chopped
½ C.   string beans or snow peas, cut into ¼-inch wide strips

Soy-Lime Sauce
3 T.   fresh lime juice
2 T.   soy sauce
1½ tsp. curry powder
1 T.   fresh Thai basil, or 1 tsp. dried basil
1 tsp.   brown sugar
¼ tsp.   sesame oil

1. Cook noodles according to directions on package, drain, set aside.
2. Mix sauce in bowl and set aside.
3. Heat oil in a 3-quart pot; add ginger, garlic, celery, green pepper, onion, sauté 3 minutes. Add beans or snow peas and sauté for an additional 1 minute. Pour sauce over vegetables. Stir. Add noodles and shrimp. Stir just to heat shrimp.

Substitutions: cooked crab, crawfish meat

Nutrients Per Serving:

Calories	245
Omega-3s	403mg
Total Fat	4g
Saturated Fat	1g
Protein	25g
Total Carbohydrate	25g
Cholesterol	221mg
Sodium	890mg
Fiber	2g

Smoked Salmon Pasta

Prep Time	Cook Time	Yields
5-10 minutes	10-15 minutes	4 servings

½ lb.	smoked salmon, broken into bite-size pieces
8 oz.	fettuccine noodles
2 T.	olive oil
1 T.	butter
1	garlic clove, minced
¼ C.	sun-dried tomatoes
1	lemon, juiced
2 T.	parsley
1½ T.	lemon zest
1 tsp.	oregano
1 C.	milk, low-fat
¼ C.	parsley, chopped

1. Cook fettuccine according to directions on package. Drain.
2. Simmer in oil and butter, garlic, tomatoes, lemon juice, parsley, zest, oregano, milk, over medium heat while fettuccine is cooking.
3. Toss sauce with drained pasta.
4. Crumble smoked salmon over pasta.
5. Garnish with chopped parsley.

Substitutions: smoked tuna, trout, leftover grilled salmon

Nutrients Per Serving:

Calories	364
Omega-3s	294mg
Total Fat	13g
Saturated Fat	3g
Protein	16g
Total Carbohydrate	47g
Cholesterol	18mg
Sodium	505mg
Fiber	2g

Spaghetti with Clams

Digging clams is a fun family activity. Razor clams from the Pacific and off the coast of France are my favorites. They are an excellent source of vitamin B12, iron and selenium.

Prep Time	Cook Time	Yields
5-10 minutes	15-20 minutes	6 servings

2	10.5 oz. cans baby clams, drained, rinsed
12 oz.	spaghetti noodles
1 T.	olive oil
1	large onion, finely chopped
1	garlic clove, minced
1	14.5 oz. can tomatoes, crushed, undrained
1 T.	tomato paste
½ tsp.	dried oregano
½ tsp.	dried rosemary
Pepper, to taste	
1 T.	fresh parsley, chopped

1. Boil spaghetti noodles according to directions on package.
2. Heat oil in a large saucepan. Add onion and garlic and sauté for 5 minutes, until softened. Add tomatoes and tomato paste, oregano, rosemary and pepper.
3. Bring to boil, reduce heat, simmer for 15 minutes.
4. Stir in clams, heat for 2 minutes or until very hot.
5. Toss well with hot spaghetti and sprinkle with parsley before serving.

Substitutions: cooked shrimp or canned tuna

Nutrients Per Serving:

Calories	378
Omega-3s	263mg
Total Fat	5g
Saturated Fat	1g
Protein	28g
Total Carbohydrate	55g
Cholesterol	56mg
Sodium	217mg
Fiber	3g

Chapter 10

Finfish Entrees

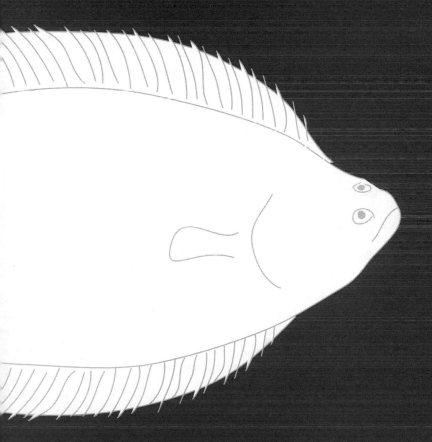

Award-Winning Cod in Phyllo

I won my first cooking contest with this recipe. I developed it using cod from America's first frozen-at-sea catcher processor, the Arctic Trawler. The flash frozen cod fillets were of fantastic quality but the boat owner couldn't sell the catch. Giving cod the award-winning honor it deserved brought chefs to his galley door. The distinguished panel of judges couldn't believe that the cod fish was frozen.

Prep Time	Cook Time	Yields
20-25 minutes	35-40 minutes	4 servings

4   cod fillets (4-oz.ea.), boneless, skinless
Salt and pepper to taste
2 T. butter
2 tsp. Bouquet Garni
2   garlic cloves, finely minced

1 C. sautéed vegetables (any combination of chopped onions, celery, bell peppers, mushrooms)
1 C. sharp cheddar, grated
12   sheets of phyllo dough
olive oil spray

1. Preheat oven to 350°F.
2. Pat cod very dry with paper towels.
3. Season cod with salt and pepper.
4. Melt butter in a saucepan, add Bouquet Garni and garlic. Set aside.
5. Sauté vegetables in a small pan (or use leftovers, warmed). Set aside.

To make phyllo wrapped cod
1. Use three sheets of phyllo dough per fillet.
2. Lay phyllo dough on a flat surface and coat each layer with olive oil and melted butter.
3. Position fillet in center of each 3 sheet stack of phyllo dough.
4. Place ¼ C. sautéed vegetables on top of fish and top with ¼ C. cheddar cheese.
5. Fold sides of dough over fish, roll packet up like an egg roll.
6. Spray outside of dough with olive oil.
7. Repeat to make four phyllo packets.
8. Bake on an oiled baking pan at 350°F. for 30 minutes.

Tip: *Delicious using salmon.*

Nutrients Per Serving:

Calories	416
Omega-3s	356mg
Total Fat	17g
Saturated Fat	9g
Protein	30g
Total Carbohydrate	33g
Cholesterol	80mg
Sodium	693mg
Fiber	2g

Baked Flounder with Seasoned Crumbs

Prep Time	Cook Time	Yields
5-10 minutes	25 minutes	4 servings

4	5 oz. flounder fillets, boneless, skinless
1 T.	olive oil
1 T.	Dijon mustard
¾ C.	coarse, dry breadcrumbs
2 T.	fresh parsley, chopped
1	onion, chopped
3	tomatoes, chopped
⅓ C.	dry white wine or chicken broth

salt to taste
vegetable oil spray

1. Preheat oven to 400°F.
2. Mix oil, mustard, breadcrumbs, parsley in a small bowl. Set aside.
3. Preheat a large, ovenproof skillet on medium heat. Oil skillet. Add onion. Sauté 6 minutes. Add tomatoes and wine, stirring constantly, for 3 minutes.
4. Arrange fillets in a single layer over vegetable mixture and season with salt.
5. Sprinkle breadcrumb mixture evenly over fillets. Gently press crumbs into fillet.
6. Bake uncovered for 20 minutes or until internal temperature of fish reaches 145° F.

Substitutions: sole, perch, striped bass

Nutrients Per Serving:

Calories	274
Omega-3s	306mg
Total Fat	5g
Saturated Fat	2g
Protein	29g
Total Carbohydrate	23g
Cholesterol	69mg
Sodium	341mg
Fiber	3g

Basil Baked Halibut in Foil Packets

Baking fish in sealed foil is actually steam cooking the fish. It's great on the grill, too.

Prep Time	Cook Time	Yields
10-15 minutes	15-20 minutes	4 servings

1 lb.	halibut fillet
2 T.	olive oil
1	garlic clove, finely minced
½ C.	fresh basil, finely minced
3 T.	fresh lemon juice
salt and pepper, to taste	
¼ C.	red bell pepper, minced

1. Preheat oven to 450°F.
2. Mix olive oil, garlic, basil, lemon juice in a bowl.
3. Cut foil large enough to cover fillet, allowing ample foil for folding top and ends.
4. Lay fish on foil, pull up sides and pour basil oil over fish. Season with salt and pepper.
5. Tightly fold foil around fish. Place packets on a cookie sheet.
6. Bake packets for 12 minutes, or until internal temperature reaches 145° F.
7. Carefully open foil and garnish with red bell peppers.

Substitutions: haddock, bass, mackerel

Tip: *Foil packets are good for lots of reasons – they're festive, make for easy clean-up and create a delicious dinner.*

Nutrients Per Serving:

Calories	190
Omega-3s	541mg
Total Fat	10g
Saturated Fat	2g
Protein	24g
Total Carbohydrate	2g
Cholesterol	36mg
Sodium	120mg
Fiber	1g

Baked Salmon Parmesan

Prep Time	Cook Time	Yields
5 minutes	12 minutes	4 servings

1 lb.   salmon, cut into four serving pieces
⅓ C.   low-fat mayonnaise
¼ C. plus 2 T. Parmesan cheese, grated
½   small onion, finely chopped
1   garlic clove, minced
2 T.   fresh parsley, chopped
⅛ tsp. salt and pepper
garnish with lemon wedges

1. Preheat oven to 450°F. Oil a baking sheet.
2. Mix mayonnaise, ¼ C. Parmesan cheese, onion, garlic, parsley, salt, pepper in a small bowl.
3. Lay salmon on a baking sheet. Spread mixture evenly over salmon.
4. Sprinkle remaining Parmesan on top.
5. Bake uncovered for 12 minutes, or until salmon reaches the internal temperature of 145° F.

Tip: *Serve over rice or noodles with lemon wedges.*

Substitutions: mahi-mahi, tuna, swordfish

Nutrients Per Serving:

Calories	275
Omega-3s	1,423mg
Total Fat	16g
Saturated Fat	4g
Protein	28g
Total Carbohydrate	4g
Cholesterol	64mg
Sodium	401mg
Fiber	1g

Sumptuous Seafood Bake

This family favorite is served quite often for brunch.

Prep Time	Cook Time	Yields
10-15 minutes	40 minutes	8 servings

1 lb.	cod, cubed, boneless, skinless
	vegetable cooking spray
8	slices whole-grain bread, cubed
1	onion, chopped
1 C.	celery, chopped
1	red bell pepper, chopped
⅓ C.	low-fat mayonnaise
4	eggs
3 C.	low-fat milk
1	10.75 oz. can fat-free cream of mushroom soup
½ C.	cheddar cheese, grated (optional)

1. Preheat oven to 450°F. Coat a casserole dish with cooking oil.
2. Evenly arrange half of bread in bottom of casserole dish.
3. Mix fish, onion, celery, pepper and mayonnaise in a bowl. Spread over the bread.
4. Evenly arrange remaining bread over top of fish mixture.
5. Beat eggs, milk, soup in a bowl. Pour mixture over bread.
6. Bake uncovered for 15 minutes. Reduce oven temperature to 350° F. Bake for 20 minutes.
7. Sprinkle with cheese and bake 5 minutes.

Substitutions: shrimp and crab meat, extra small oysters, tilapia

Nutrients Per Serving:

Calories	305
Omega-3s	190mg
Total Fat	11g
Saturated Fat	3g
Protein	20g
Total Carbohydrate	30g
Cholesterol	138mg
Sodium	723mg
Fiber	2g

Baked Whitefish Au Gratin

Prep Time	Cook Time	Yields
5-10 minutes	10 minutes	4 servings

1 lb.	whitefish, boneless, skinless
1	red bell pepper, finely chopped
3	stalks celery, finely chopped
1	small onion, finely chopped
1 C.	toasted breadcrumbs
⅓ C.	low-fat mayonnaise
2 T.	fresh lemon juice

salt and pepper to taste

Topping

½ C.	cheddar cheese, grated (optional)
½ C.	slivered almonds (optional)

garnish with paprika

1. Preheat oven to 450°F.
2. Combine all ingredients except topping in a 1½ -quart baking dish.
3. Bake for 20 minutes.
4. Sprinkle with toppings.
5. Bake additional 10 minutes.

Substitutions: sole, catfish, tilapia

Nutrients Per Serving:

Calories	279
Omega-3s	843mg
Total Fat	12g
Saturated Fat	2g
Protein	15g
Total Carbohydrate	29g
Cholesterol	39mg
Sodium	557mg
Fiber	3g

Broiled Catfish with Pecorino Romano

A *skinless fillet has two sides, the skin side and the presentation side. The skin side usually has a little darker meat where the fat lies between the skin and meat. Place the skin side up first on a broiler or grill. Half way through cooking, turn and finish with the presentation side up.*

Prep Time	Cook Time	Yields
5-10 minutes	10-12 minutes	4 servings

1 lb.   catfish fillets, boneless, skinless
2 tsp. lemon juice
salt and pepper

Topping

¼ C.   low-fat mayonnaise
2 T.   Pecorino Romano cheese, grated
2   green onions, sliced
2   garlic cloves, minced
2 tsp. fresh lemon juice
1 tsp. Dijon mustard
¼ tsp. Tabasco sauce (or to taste)

1. Adjust oven rack to 4-inches below top of oven. Preheat on broil.
2. Mix topping ingredients in a small bowl and set aside.
3. Place presentation side of fish on oiled, foil lined broiling pan.
4. Sprinkle with lemon juice and salt and pepper.
5. Broil 3 minutes, turn and cook until internal temperature reaches 140°F.
6. Remove fish from oven, spread topping evenly over fish. Broil for 1 minute or until golden brown.

Substitutions: trout, halibut, flounder

Nutrients Per Serving:

Calories	255
Omega-3s	734mg
Total Fat	10g
Saturated Fat	2g
Protein	37g
Total Carbohydrate	3g
Cholesterol	62mg
Sodium	399mg
Fiber	1g

Broiled Herb-Coated Salmon

I prefer skin-on fillets for broiling. The skin gives extra protection from the intense broiler heat and adds more flavor.

Prep Time	Cook Time	Yields
5-10 minutes	10 minutes	6 servings

2 lb.   salmon fillet, skin-on
1 T.   olive oil
Pinch salt

Spice rub
4 T.   fresh basil, chopped
2 T.   fresh parsley, chopped
1 T.   fresh rosemary, chopped
1 tsp.   lemon pepper seasoning

Tip: *If the fish fillet is 1/2-inch thick or less, you don't need to turn it.*

1. Adjust oven rack to 6-inches below top of oven. Preheat on broil.
2. Mix spice rub in a small bowl.
3. Lay fish skin side up on oiled, foil lined broiler pan.
4. Broil 3 minutes. Turn.
5. Coat top of fish with olive oil, season with salt. Evenly rub in spice mixture over top of salmon.
6. Broil until thickest part of fish reaches 145°F.

Substitutions: flounder, trout, Arctic char

Nutrients Per Serving:

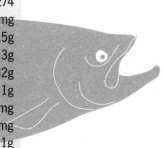

Calories	274
Omega-3s	1919mg
Total Fat	15g
Saturated Fat	3g
Protein	32g
Total Carbohydrate	1g
Cholesterol	99mg
Sodium	171mg
Fiber	1g

Broiled Lingcod
with Miso Glaze

Miso is widely used in Asian cooking. It is a cultured soybean paste that gives a wonderful sweetness. Miso is also tasty in seafood soup and salad dressing.

Prep Time	Cook Time	Yields
35 minutes	7 minutes	4 servings

4	6 oz. lingcod fillets, skin-on
1 T.	olive oil
1 T.	soy sauce
1 T.	fresh ginger root, peeled and minced
1½ T.	sesame seeds (optional)
oil	

Miso Glaze

¼ C.	miso, such as Westbrae Natural Organic Mellow White Miso
2 T.	dry white wine or broth
1 T.	olive oil
1 T.	honey
1 T.	fresh lemon juice
1	garlic clove, minced

1. Mix one tablespoon olive oil, soy sauce, ginger in a small bowl.
2. Pour over fish in a baking dish; turn fish to coat well. Cover. Marinate for 30 minutes.
3. Mix miso glaze ingredients in a bowl.
4. Pre-heat broiler. Line broiler pan with foil. Spray foil with oil.
5. Place fish on foil skin side up. Broil 4 inches from heat source for 2 minutes.
6. Turn fish and spread miso glaze evenly over top.
7. Broil until fish reaches internal temperature of 145° F. at thickest part, about 5 minutes.

Substitutions: bass, grouper, haddock

Nutrients Per Serving:

Calories	139
Omega-3s	235mg
Total Fat	5g
Saturated Fat	2g
Protein	29g
Total Carbohydrate	23g
Cholesterol	169mg
Sodium	341mg
Fiber	3g

Broiled Striped Bass with Moroccan Herb Sauce

Prep Time	Cook Time	Yields
5-10 minutes	5 minutes	6 servings

1 ½ lbs. bass fillets
Vegetable oil spray

Moroccan Herb Sauce
½ C.	fresh parsley, minced
½ C.	fresh cilantro, minced
¼ C.	olive oil
2	garlic cloves, minced
1	lemon, grated zest and juice
1 tsp.	ground cumin
1 tsp.	paprika
½ tsp.	salt
½ tsp.	ground coriander
Pinch	cayenne pepper

1. Mix sauce ingredients in a gallon food-grade self sealing bag. Place fish in bag. Refrigerate. Marinate 30 minutes or overnight.
2. Adjust oven rack to 4-inches from heat source. Pre-heat broiler. Line broiler pan with oil-sprayed foil.
3. Lay fish on foil.
4. Broil 4 minutes, turn and cook until fish reaches internal temperature of 145°F.
5. Serve with rice and steamed carrots.

Substitutions: tilapia, catfish, salmon. Use any combination of fresh herbs: basil, thyme, oregano, mint

Nutrients Per Serving:
Calories	233
Omega-3s	627mg
Total Fat	12g
Saturated Fat	2g
Protein	29g
Total Carbohydrate	3g
Cholesterol	53mg
Sodium	196mg
Fiber	1g

Cajun-Style Snapper

Prep Time	Cook Time	Yields
5 minutes	8 minutes	4 servings

4 6 oz. snapper fillets
vegetable cooking spray

Spice Rub
1 tsp.   mustard powder
1 tsp.   ground cumin
1 tsp.   paprika
½ tsp.   garlic powder
½ tsp.   cayenne pepper
½ tsp.   dried thyme
½ tsp.   dried oregano

1. Pat fish very dry with paper towels.
2. Mix spice rub ingredients in a bowl. Rub spices on both sides of fish, coat well.
3. Heat skillet to medium high. Spray both sides of fish with vegetable oil cooking spray. Lay fillet in skillet.
4. Turn heat down to medium low. Cook fish 4 minutes, turn. Cook 4 more minutes.

Substitutions: tilapia, catfish, pollock

Nutrients Per Serving:

Calories	175
Omega-3s	372mg
Total Fat	4g
Saturated Fat	1g
Protein	31g
Total Carbohydrate	2g
Cholesterol	74mg
Sodium	99mg
Fiber	1g

Cheese Crumbed Sole with Salad Greens

To make a crispier fish fillet when broiling, place it on a wire cooling rack so the hot oven air will surround and penetrate the entire piece of seafood.

Prep Time	Cook Time	Yields
10-15 minutes	5 minutes	4 servings

4	4 oz. sole fillets
1 T.	Dijon mustard
1	egg white
1 C.	fresh breadcrumbs
¼ C.	Parmesan cheese, grated
1 tsp.	lemon peel, grated
2 tsp.	olive oil
½ tsp.	salt
3 C.	romaine lettuce, chopped
3	Roma tomatoes, chopped
¼ C.	fresh basil, finely chopped
1 T.	balsamic vinegar

1. Adjust oven rack to 6-inches from heat source. Preheat broiler. Line broiler pan with foil.
2. Mix mustard and egg white in a shallow bowl.
3. Mix breadcrumbs, Parmesan cheese, lemon peel in another bowl.
4. Pat fish dry with paper towels. Dip in egg white mixture, turning to coat well.
5. Coat fish in breadcrumb mixture.
6. Lay sole on oiled cookie rack. Place rack on top of foil on broiler pan. Broil for 4 minutes, or until fish reaches internal temperature of 145° F. Watch carefully.
7. Mix vinegar, oil, salt in a small bowl. Divide lettuce, tomatoes, basil onto 4 serving plates, sprinkle vinegar over greens and top with broiled fish.

Substitutions: trout, tilapia, catfish

Nutrients Per Serving:

Calories	325
Omega-3s	141mg
Total Fat	10g
Saturated Fat	2g
Protein	32g
Total Carbohydrate	27g
Cholesterol	6mg
Sodium	548mg
Fiber	3g

Crusty Halibut Bake

Prep Time	Cook Time	Yields
2 hours	15 minutes	4 servings

1 lb.	halibut fillets
1 C.	white wine or broth
½ tsp.	salt
⅓ C.	low-fat mayonnaise
⅓ C.	low-fat sour cream
¼ C.	green onions, sliced
1 C.	corn flakes, crushed very fine
½ tsp.	paprika

1. Marinate halibut in wine for 2 hours in refrigerator.
2. When ready to bake, preheat oven to 450°F.
3. Drain marinade and pat fish dry with paper towels. Lay fish in a baking dish. Salt fish.
4. Mix mayonnaise, sour cream, onions in a small bowl; spread evenly over fish.
5. Sprinkle fish evenly with cornflakes. Dust with paprika.
6. Bake uncovered for 15 minutes, or until fish reaches an internal temperature of 145° F.

Substitutions: barramundi, haddock, trout

Tip: *Put cornflakes in a plastic bag, seal and crush. This keeps the little bits from flying around. If you don't have a rolling pin, crush them with an unopened soup can.*

Nutrients Per Serving:

Calories	286
Omega-3s	522mg
Total Fat	12g
Saturated Fat	3g
Protein	25g
Total Carbohydrate	9g
Cholesterol	51mg
Sodium	865mg
Fiber	1g

Grandma's Salmon Biscuit Bake

Prep Time	Cook Time	Yields
5-10 minutes	25-30 minutes	5 servings

1	**7 oz. can salmon, drained, skin removed**
½ C.	**celery, chopped**
2 T.	**sweet onion, chopped**
2 T.	**red bell pepper, diced**
2 T.	**butter**
¼ C.	**flour**
1¼ C.	**low-fat milk**
1 C.	**peas**
½ C.	**mushrooms, sliced**
2 T.	**fresh parsley, chopped**
¼ tsp.	**salt**
¼ tsp.	**dried thyme**
pinch	**cayenne pepper**
1 pkg.	**refigerated buttermilk biscuits**

1. Preheat oven to 450°F.
2. Sauté celery, onion, bell pepper in butter over medium heat about 5 minutes. Slowly sprinkle flour over vegetables to prevent lumps. Slowly stir in milk to prevent lumps. Add peas, mushrooms, parsley and spices. Stir until sauce is thick. Do not boil.
3. Flake salmon into sauce. Gently mix. Pour into an oiled 1½-qt oven-proof dish.
4. Top with biscuits. Bake for 15 minutes, or until biscuits are browned.

Substitutions: cooked crawfish, crab, shrimp meat

Nutrients Per Serving:

Calories	277
Omega-3s	435mg
Total Fat	10g
Saturated Fat	4g
Protein	15g
Total Carbohydrate	33g
Cholesterol	32mg
Sodium	749mg
Fiber	3g

Halibut Cordon Bleu

Prep Time	Cook Time	Yields
5-10 minutes	15 minutes	4 servings

1 lb.	halibut, thick fillet, boneless, skinless
4 tsp.	Dijon mustard
4 oz.	Swiss cheese, sliced
2 slices	honey-baked ham, thinly sliced
4 tsp.	low-fat mayonnaise
¼ C.	breadcrumbs

1. Preheat oven to 450°F.
2. Cut fish fillet horizontally in half, through middle, leaving one side connected (a book cut).
3. Open up fillet and spread mustard over inside, layer with ham and cheese slices.
4. Close fish.
5. Spread top of fish with mayonnaise and sprinkle with breadcrumbs.
6. Bake uncovered for 15 minutes, or until fish reaches internal temperature of 145° F.

Substitutions: salmon, swordfish, grouper

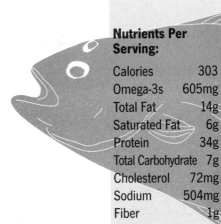

Nutrients Per Serving:

Calories	303
Omega-3s	605mg
Total Fat	14g
Saturated Fat	6g
Protein	34g
Total Carbohydrate	7g
Cholesterol	72mg
Sodium	504mg
Fiber	1g

Heavenly Halibut Casserole

Prep Time	Cook Time	Yields
5-10 minutes	35 minutes	6 servings

1½ lb.   halibut fillets, boneless, skinless
2 tsp.   Old Bay seasoning
1 C.   onions, chopped
1 C.   cheddar or Monterey cheese, grated
1   10.75 oz. can condensed, reduced sodium, cream of mushroom soup
¼ C.   low-fat sour cream
¼ C.   low-fat mayonnaise
½ C.   water
Lemon wedges, to serve

Tip: To make fresh, better-than-store-bought Old Bay seasoning, see the recipe on page 219.

1. Preheat oven to 450°F.
2. Lay fish in an ovenproof large baking dish. Sprinkle with Old Bay.
3. Top with onions.
4. Sprinkle with cheese.
5. Combine soup, sour cream, mayonnaise, water in small bowl. Mix well. Evenly coat fish with sauce.
6. Cover baking dish with foil. Bake for 35 minutes.

Substitutions: boneless, skinless salmon, rockfish, catfish, scallops

Nutrients Per Serving:

Calories	319
Omega-3s	570mg
Total Fat	17g
Saturated Fat	6g
Protein	30g
Total Carbohydrate	10g
Cholesterol	62mg
Sodium	871mg
Fiber	1g

Herb-Crusted Pan-Fried Perch

Prep Time	Cook Time	Yields
10-15 minutes	6-9 minutes	4 servings

1 lb.	perch fillets
2 C.	very fine, fresh breadcrumbs
2 T.	fresh thyme, finely chopped
2 T.	fresh rosemary, finely chopped
2 T.	fresh parsley, finely chopped
½ tsp.	salt
¼ tsp.	pepper
1	egg, well beaten
1 T.	water
2 T.	oil

1. Mix breadcrumbs, herbs, salt and pepper on a plate.
2. Mix egg and water in another flat container.
3. Pat fish very dry with paper towels.
4. Dip each fillet in egg, then into breadcrumb mixture, pressing crumbs into fish to make them stick. Coat well.
5. Heat oil in a skillet on medium-high, put in fish, immediately turn down to medium-low.
6. Cook fish for 3-4 minutes on each side, or until internal temperature reaches 145° F.

Substitutions: tilapia, cod, flounder, sole

Tip: *If you don't have fresh herbs use 2 teaspoons dried.*

Nutrients Per Serving:

Calories	342
Omega-3s	502mg
Total Fat	18g
Saturated Fat	4g
Protein	23g
Total Carbohydrate	20g
Cholesterol	106mg
Sodium	567mg
Fiber	2g

Indian-Style Baked Halibut with Yogurt Sauce

On larger fish like halibut, the cheeks contain very sweet, highly prized meat.

Prep Time	Cook Time	Yields
overnight	12-15 minutes	4 servings

1 ½ lbs. halibut fillets

Yogurt Sauce

1 C.	low-fat, plain yogurt
1	serrano pepper, seeded, finely minced
¼ C.	fresh mint or dill, finely minced
2 T.	fresh cilantro, chopped
2 T.	fresh lime juice
1	garlic clove, minced
1 tsp.	fresh ginger root, grated
1 tsp.	ground cumin
½ tsp.	turmeric
¼ tsp.	salt

Tip: Use the whey (the leftover liquid in the bowl that is full of nutrients) to make a nutritious bowl of rice. Use whey in place of water; cook and season as normal.

1. Place yogurt in strainer lined with cheesecloth in a bowl, drain, cover, refrigerate overnight.
2. Mix drained yogurt (now cheese) in a medium bowl with all sauce ingredients. Refrigerate, covered, for 30 minutes to blend flavors.
3. Preheat oven to 400°F.
4. Line a baking dish with foil. Oil and place halibut on it.
5. Pour half of yogurt sauce over fillet, reserving remaining sauce for serving.
6. Bake uncovered for 12-15 minutes, or until fish reaches internal temperature of 145° F.
7. Serve with remaining yogurt sauce.

Substitutions: grouper, swordfish, striped bass

Nutrients Per Serving:

Calories	234
Omega-3s	747mg
Total Fat	5g
Saturated Fat	1g
Protein	39g
Total Carbohydrate	6g
Cholesterol	58mg
Sodium	283mg
Fiber	1g

Mahi-Mahi Fish Tacos

Fish tacos started as a regional food favorite in Southern California and Hawaii. Now they are popular all across the country! Use local fish such as cod, pollock, halibut or shrimp. Whatever fish you choose, be sure it is boneless and skinless.

Prep Time	Cook Time	Yields
15-20 minutes	8-10 minutes	8 servings

1 lb.	mahi-mahi, boneless, skinless, cut into 8 pieces
½ C.	flour
1 tsp.	cayenne pepper
¼ tsp.	salt
2 T.	vegetable oil
8	corn tortillas
4 C.	cabbage, finely shredded
3	tomatoes, diced
1 C.	cheddar cheese, grated
1	avocado, diced

Taco Sauce

½ C.	plain, low-fat yogurt
½ C.	low-fat mayonnaise
2 T.	fresh lime juice (from 1 lime)
1	jalapeño pepper, seeded, minced
1 tsp.	cayenne pepper
½ tsp.	dried oregano
½ tsp.	ground cumin
½ tsp.	dried dill

1. Mix taco sauce. Refrigerate and allow flavors to blend. (Can be made a day ahead.)
2. Pat fish dry with paper towel.
3. Mix flour, cayenne pepper, salt. Coat fish with flour mixture.
4. Heat oil on medium-high in a pan. Fry fish in oil for 2 minutes, turn and finish cooking until golden brown and reaches internal temperature of 145° F.
5. Warm tortillas on a plate in microwave for 20-30 seconds.
6. Fill taco with piece of fish, vegetables and cheese. Add sauce on top and enjoy.

Tip: *Bake tortillas in a 400°F. oven instead of microwave to make slightly crispy and browned. Keep your eye on them to make sure they don't burn!*

Nutrients Per Serving:

Calories	360
Omega-3s	251mg
Total Fat	18g
Saturated Fat	5g
Protein	19g
Total Carbohydrate	33g
Cholesterol	43mg
Sodium	338mg
Fiber	5g

Mediterranean-Style Grouper

Prep Time	Cook Time	Yields
5-10 minutes	15-20 minutes	4 servings

1 lb.	grouper fillets, boneless, skinless, cut in 4 pieces
1	medium sweet onion, diced
4	garlic cloves, sliced
2 T.	olive oil
1	14.5 oz. can diced tomatoes, undrained
1 tsp.	dried basil or oregano
¼ tsp.	lemon-pepper seasoning
¼ C.	kalamata olives, halved
2 oz.	feta cheese, crumbled

1. Sauté onion and garlic in a large skillet in olive oil until tender, about 5 minutes. Stir in tomatoes, basil, seasoning. Bring to boil, reduce heat to simmer. Simmer for 5 minutes.
2. Lay grouper in skillet. Spoon vegetables on top of fish.
3. Cover and simmer for 10 minutes. Do not stir.
4. Place grouper on serving plate.
5. Garnish with olives and feta cheese.

Substitutions: tuna, sea scallops, halibut cheeks

Nutrients Per Serving:

Calories	297
Omega-3s	585mg
Total Fat	13g
Saturated Fat	3g
Protein	28g
Total Carbohydrate	14g
Cholesterol	49mg
Sodium	522mg
Fiber	3g

Microwave Cod with Lemon Zest

Prep Time	Cook Time	Yields
5-10 minutes	10-15 minutes	4 servings

1 lb.   cod fillets, cut in 4 pieces

Marinade
¼ C.   fresh lemon juice
2 T.   olive oil
1 T.   fresh parsley, chopped
1 T.   lemon zest, finely grated
½ tsp.   chili powder
½ tsp.   salt
garnish (see tip)

1. Mix marinade ingredients in microwave proof dish.
2. Lay cod with thickest part of fillet towards outside of dish. Coat both sides of fish with marinade. Cover dish with microwave proof wrap.
3. Marinate in refrigerator for 30 minutes.
4. Remove from refrigerator. Microwave on medium 4-6 minutes or until fish reaches internal temperature of 145°F.

Substitutions: catfish, tilapia, sole

Tip: *Take time to garnish your seafood dishes. Top your dish with a medley of colorful, crunchy, chopped bell peppers, tomatoes or both.*

Nutrients Per Serving:

Calories	159
Omega-3s	269mg
Total Fat	8g
Saturated Fat	1g
Protein	20g
Total Carbohydrate	2g
Cholesterol	49mg
Sodium	356mg
Fiber	1g

Oven-Roasted Swordfish

This recipe is great for low-fat fish. The vegetables protect the fish from drying out by releasing their moisture.

Prep Time	Cook Time	Yields
5-10 minutes	15-20 minutes	4 servings

1 lb.	swordfish fillet, cut in 4 pieces
1 T.	olive oil
1	red bell pepper, thinly sliced
1	sweet onion, thinly sliced
2	garlic cloves, minced
2 T.	basil, chopped

Dressing

2 T.	fresh lime juice
⅛ tsp.	salt
1 tsp.	chili powder
2 tsp.	olive oil
¾ tsp.	ground cumin
Pinch	cayenne pepper

1. Pre-heat oven to 450° F.
2. Heat oil in an oven-proof skillet over medium heat. Sauté pepper, onion, garlic and basil for 5 minutes.
3. Mix dressing ingredients in a small bowl.
4. Shove vegetable mixture to side of skillet. Place fish in skillet and spoon sautéed vegetables over top of fish.
5. Drizzle dressing over vegetables.
6. Roast, uncovered for 12 minutes.

Substitutions: halibut, catfish, grouper

Tip: Mix vegetables and herbs according to what's in the cupboard, refrigerator or in the garden. Add green beans, asparagus, dill, cilantro, or other family favorites.

Nutrients Per Serving:

Calories	220
Omega-3s	607mg
Total Fat	6g
Saturated Fat	1g
Protein	36g
Total Carbohydrate	4g
Cholesterol	63mg
Sodium	203mg
Fiber	1g

Pan-Fried Catfish on Spinach Greens

Prep Time	Cook Time	Yields
10-15 minutes	10-15 minutes	4 servings

1½ lb. catfish fillets
vegetable cooking spray
1 strip bacon, chopped
2 T. sweet onion, chopped
1 T. red wine vinegar
1 T. fresh lemon juice
4 C. baby spinach leaves, washed
2 T. olive oil
Salt and pepper to taste

Cajun Spice Rub
1 T. sweet paprika
1 tsp. ground fennel seeds
1 tsp. dried thyme
1 tsp. black pepper
½ tsp. cayenne pepper

1. Pre-heat oven to 200° F. Place oven-proof serving plate in oven.
2. Mix spice rub in a small bowl.
3. Pat fish fillets very dry with a paper towel. Coat fish with vegetable cooking spray.
4. Press each side of fillet with Cajun rub. Set aside.
5. Place bacon and onion in skillet and cook until bacon is crisp. Turn heat down to low.
6. Add vinegar and lemon juice to skillet, stir, add spinach. Toss to slightly wilt.
7. Transfer spinach to a warmed serving plate. Return plate to oven.
8. Add oil to a skillet and heat to medium-high.
9. Fry catfish for 4 minutes, turn and cook until internal temperature reaches 145° F.
10. Lay catfish on top of spinach. Salt and pepper to taste.

Substitutions: tilapia, mahi-mahi, scallops

Nutrients Per Serving:

Calories	353
Omega-3s	724mg
Total Fat	25g
Saturated Fat	5g
Protein	29g
Total Carbohydrate	4g
Cholesterol	86mg
Sodium	311mg
Fiber	2g

Pan-Fried Trout in Sage

Prep Time	Cook Time	Yields
5-10 minutes	10-15 minutes	4 servings

4	8 oz. whole trout, cleaned, rinsed
8	large fresh sage leaves
½ C.	cornmeal
¼ tsp.	cayenne pepper
1 strip	bacon
2 T.	olive oil
2 T.	butter
1	lemon, juiced

leaves from 4 large sage sprigs
salt and pepper to taste

Tip: *Use herbs grown in your region such as rosemary, savory, oregano, or thyme.*

1. Preheat oven to 200°F. Warm an ovenproof plate.
2. Pat trout very dry with paper towels.
3. Season inside of each trout with salt and pepper. Place a sage leaf inside each fish.
4. Mix cornmeal, cayenne, a shake of salt in flat container. Roll outside of fish in cornmeal. Coat well. Set aside.
5. Cook bacon in a large skillet until crisp; transfer to paper towels. Crumble when cooled.
6. Add olive oil to bacon oil. Heat oil and fry trout, cooking until fish reaches an internal temperature of 145°F. Transfer to warmed plate.
7. Pour off most of fat in skillet and add butter.
8. Cook sage sprigs over medium-high heat for two minutes, until leaves are crisp.
9. Add lemon juice to sage mixture in skillet. Scrape bottom of skillet, stir, pour over trout.
10. Top with crumbled bacon. Serve immediately.

Substitutions: perch, mullet, tilapia

Nutrients Per Serving:

Calories	455
Omega-3s	1,768mg
Total Fat	27g
Saturated Fat	8g
Protein	38g
Total Carbohydrate	14g
Cholesterol	123mg
Sodium	333mg
Fiber	2g

Poached Salmon Steaks in Lemon-Thyme Broth

I like cooking seafood steaks because the skin and bone adds flavor and quite often is less expensive than a fillet. After cooking, it is easy to remove the skin and bone and serve a tasty boneless salmon meal.

Prep Time	Cook Time	Yields
5-10 minutes	10-15 minutes	4 servings

4	6 oz. salmon steaks
2	lemons, juice and zest
4 C.	low-sodium chicken broth
3	garlic cloves, sliced
8 sprigs fresh thyme (or 1 T. dried)	
10	whole black peppercorns
1 T.	olive oil
½ tsp.	salt

1. Remove zest from lemons using a vegetable peeler.
2. Juice lemons, place juice and zest in a deep pot.
3. Add broth, garlic, thyme, peppercorns. Bring to a boil.
4. Turn heat down and simmer for 5 minutes.
5. Add steaks to pot; cover and simmer on low.
6. Check fish after 8 minutes. Fish is done when internal temperature reaches 145° F.
7. Remove fish with slotted spatula from broth, drizzle with olive oil, season with salt.

Substitutions: halibut, snapper, swordfish

Tip: *Refrigerate broth for tomorrow's start on seafood soup.*

Nutrients Per Serving:

Calories	241
Omega-3s	760mg
Total Fat	7g
Saturated Fat	1g
Protein	39g
Total Carbohydrate	3g
Cholesterol	54mg
Sodium	867mg
Fiber	1g

Poor Man's Lobster

This was one of the most requested recipes from my weekly TV seafood cooking show in Seattle.

Prep Time	Cook Time	Yields
5 minutes	10 minutes	4 servings

1 lb.	halibut, boneless, skinless fillet, cut into 2x4-inch rectangles
½ C.	sugar
½ C.	vinegar
2 T.	salt
4 qt.	water
½ tsp.	parsley, chopped
⅛ tsp.	paprika

Tip: *Stretch your seafood by mixing cooked halibut and crab meat. Refrigerate over night and the halibut takes on the flavor of the crab.*

1. Preheat oven to 200°F. Warm an ovenproof serving dish.
2. Mix sugar, vinegar, salt, water in a pot. Bring to a boil.
3. Add halibut in small batches and continue boiling.
4. Remove halibut with a slotted spoon from water after 2 minutes. Place on paper towel lined, warmed serving dish. Start another batch.
5. Sprinkle with parsley and paprika. Sure, go ahead, melt some butter!

Substitutions: mahi-mahi, tuna, monkfish

Nutrients Per Serving:

Calories	111
Omega-3s	245mg
Total Fat	1g
Saturated Fat	0g
Protein	12g
Total Carbohydrate	13g
Cholesterol	18g
Sodium	551g
Fiber	0g

Roasted King Salmon on a Wood Baking Plank

Roasting fish on a wood baking plank is a traditional cooking method found world-wide. Most cultures use a local wood to create smoke to flavor food. Northwest Native Americans use alder, Hawaiians use kiawe, Southwest Natives use mesquite. Throughout the world you'll find a traditional smoke flavor!

Prep Time	Cook Time	Yields
5-10 minute	15-20 minutes	4 servings

4	5 oz. king salmon fillets, boneless
1	wood roasting plank
1 T.	olive oil
	salt and pepper
	lemon wedges, to serve

Cucumber-Dill Sauce

½ C.	low-fat sour cream
½ C.	cucumber, grated and squeezed dry
1 T.	fresh dill, chopped
1 T.	fresh lemon juice
1 tsp.	garlic, minced
	dash of hot sauce
	salt and pepper

Tip: *You don't need to soak a wood baking plank. They are extra thick.*

1. Preheat oven to 375°F. Coat salmon with olive oil.
2. Place salmon on wood roasting plank.
3. Season with salt and pepper. Cook for 20 minutes or until fish reaches internal temperature of 145° F.
4. Mix cucumber-dill sauce.
5. Serve salmon directly from oven to table accompanied with cucumber-dill sauce.

Substitutions: black cod, trout, bluefish

Nutrients Per Serving:

Calories	287
Omega-3s	1,794mg
Total Fat	15g
Saturated Fat	4g
Protein	33g
Total Carbohydrate	4g
Cholesterol	98mg
Sodium	262mg
Fiber	1g

Salmon on a Bed of Vegetables

This is a great dish for keta (or pink) salmon. The paprika livens up the meat color since these salmon tend to have lighter colored meat.

Prep Time	Cook Time	Yields
15-20 minutes	15-20 minutes	4 servings

1 lb.	salmon fillets, cut into serving sized pieces
2	carrots, peeled, thinly sliced
2	small red potatoes, thinly sliced
½	green bell pepper, cored, seeded, thinly sliced
½	onion, thinly sliced
1 T.	olive oil
¼ C.	Dijon mustard
¼ C.	fresh parsley, minced
¼ C.	fresh dill, minced
2 T.	paprika
¼ C.	sesame seeds

Salt and pepper, to taste

1. Preheat oven to 450°F.
2. Place vegetables in microwave proof bowl. Coat vegetables with olive oil, season with salt and pepper. Microwave, uncovered for 3 minutes.
3. Mix mustard, parsley, dill, paprika in a small bowl. Lay salmon in a baking dish. Spread mustard mixture evenly over salmon. Top salmon with vegetables. Sprinkle with sesame seeds.
4. Bake covered for 15 minutes, or until fish reaches internal temperature of 145° F.

Substitutions: catfish, trout, grouper

Nutrients Per Serving:

Calories	452
Omega-3s	1,421mg
Total Fat	21g
Saturated Fat	5g
Protein	29g
Total Carbohydrate	37g
Cholesterol	57mg
Sodium	455mg
Fiber	9g

Rockfish Fillets in Curry Sauce

There are 70 species of rockfish in the ocean. Rockfish generally fall into two categories: red-fleshed and brown-fleshed fillets. When pacific snapper or rockfish are in the seafood counter, the fillets are a mixture of species, hence the fillet color differences. They all taste great with this recipe.

Prep Time	Cook Time	Yields
5-10 minutes	10-15 minutes	4 servings

1 lb.   rockfish fillets, cut into 4 pieces

Sauce

2 C.	low-fat coconut milk
3 T.	curry powder
1 T.	flour
1 T.	fresh lemon juice
½ tsp.	ground cumin
½ tsp.	turmeric
½ tsp.	lemon-pepper seasoning
¼ C.	breadcrumbs
2 T.	fresh cilantro, chopped

1. Preheat oven to 450°F.
2. Whisk milk, curry powder, flour, lemon juice, cumin, turmeric and lemon-pepper in a medium bowl. Pour half of sauce in a baking dish.
3. Lay fish fillets on top of sauce and pour remaining sauce over fish. Mix cilantro and bread crumbs. Cover fish with bread crumbs.
4. Bake uncovered for 12 minutes, or until fish reaches internal temperature of 145° F.

Substitutions: mahi-mahi, snapper, cod

Tip: *Serve with hot basmati rice, a fruit plate medley of pineapple rings, mandarin oranges and bananas. Sprinkle with toasted almonds.*

Nutrients Per Serving:

Calories	200
Omega-3s	446mg
Total Fat	3g
Saturated Fat	1g
Protein	27g
Total Carbohydrate	16g
Cholesterol	42mg
Sodium	216mg
Fiber	2g

Salmon Quiche

Excellent source of vitamin B12 and selenium

Prep Time	Cook Time	Yields
20-30 minutes	55-60 minutes	12 servings

		Pastry	
2 C.	salmon, boneless, skinless, bite sized chunks		
¼ C.	sweet onion, minced		
2 T.	butter		
2 T.	sherry	**Pastry**	
2 T.	dill weed	1¾ C.	flour
4	eggs (2 whole, 2 whites)	½ tsp.	salt
½ C.	half and half cream	½ C.	cold butter, cut into cubes
½ C.	fat-free sour cream		
2 T.	light cream cheese	2 T.	shortening
¼ tsp.	each salt, white pepper, nutmeg	1	egg yolk
		3 T.	ice water
½ C.	grated Swiss cheese		

Tip: *If you don't have a pastry blender, use two forks, one in each hand, to dice up the butter. A flaky crust depends on cold butter and water.*

1. Make quiche pastry shell by blending flour and salt. Cut in cold butter and shortening with pastry blender until pieces of butter are size of peas. Add yolk and enough water to moisten dough and shape in a ball.
2. On plastic cling-wrap sheet, pat into ball, wrap tightly, refrigerate for 2 hours or overnight.
3. Preheat oven to 375°F.
4. Sprinkle counter with flour and roll dough out.
5. Fit dough to 10-inch quiche or pie pan, molding edges with your fingers. Bake for 10 minutes. Remove from oven.
6. Sauté onions in butter in a fry pan. Add salmon, sherry, dill. Gently stir.
7. Mix eggs, cream, sour cream, cream cheese, salt, pepper, nutmeg in separate bowl.
8. Carefully spoon egg mixture into salmon mixture. Gently stir.
9. Pour into pastry shell. Sprinkle cheese on top.
10. Bake at 375°F. for 35 to 40 minutes, or until top of quiche is firm.

Nutrients Per Serving:

Calories	311
Omega-3s	462mg
Total Fat	21g
Saturated Fat	9g
Protein	14g
Total Carbohydrate	17g
Cholesterol	133mg
Sodium	290mg
Fiber	1g

Substitution: crab, shrimp meat, canned salmon

Salmon Steaks with Tomato-Lime Salsa

Salmon steaks are great in the microwave because the cuts are uniform in thickness making for equal heat distribution. Tuck thin belly flap of steaks into body cavity during cooking.

Prep Time	Cook Time	Yields
5-10 minutes	10 minutes	6 servings

6	5 oz. salmon steaks, ¾-inch thick

Tomato-Lime Salsa

1 C.	zucchini, thinly sliced
3	Roma tomatoes, chopped
½ C.	green onions, chopped
2 T.	fresh cilantro, chopped
½ C.	fresh lime or lemon juice
4	garlic cloves, minced
1 tsp.	chili powder
½ tsp.	ground cumin
¼ tsp.	salt
⅛ tsp.	cayenne pepper

1. Arrange salmon in a microwavable dish, with backbone of salmon facing toward outside rim of dish.
2. Layer zucchini, tomato, green onion, cilantro, over salmon.
3. Mix lime juice, garlic, chili powder, cumin, salt, cayenne pepper in a small bowl.
4. Pour lime mixture over salmon.
5. Cover with microwave proof wrap, turn back one corner. Microwave on medium 3-4 minutes or until fish flakes with a fork. Rotate during cooking.
6. Let stand for 2 minutes before removing wrap.

Tip: *Each steak can be an individual serving, making them great for portion control.*

Nutrients Per Serving:

Calories	266
Omega-3s	1,811mg
Total Fat	13g
Saturated Fat	2g
Protein	32g
Total Carbohydrate	7g
Cholesterol	88mg
Sodium	273mg
Fiber	2g

Santa Fe Catfish

Prep Time	Cook Time	Yields
5-10 minutes	4-6 minutes	4 servings

1 lb.	catfish, cut into serving size pieces
1	tomato, chopped
¼	onion, chopped
¼ C.	cilantro, chopped
3 T.	green chilies, diced, drained
1 T.	lime juice
¼ tsp.	EACH salt, pepper, oregano

1. Place catfish in a microwave-proof dish.
2. Mix remaining ingredients in a bowl.
3. Pour over fish and cover dish.
4. Microwave on high 3-6 minutes or until fish flakes.
5. Serve with black beans and salsa.

Substitutions: cod, tilapia, bass

Nutrients Per Serving:

Calories	148
Omega-3s	450mg
Total Fat	1g
Saturated Fat	0g
Protein	17g
Total Carbohydrate	0g
Cholesterol	49 mg
Sodium	336 mg
Fiber	3g

Sautéed Sole with Pesto Wine Sauce

Treat yourself to a species of sole called Petrale. It's highly prized for having firm, sweet meat.

Prep Time	Cook Time	Yields
10-15 minutes	5-10 minutes	4 servings

4	5 oz. sole fillets
2	eggs
½ C.	milk
¼ C.	flour
1 T.	butter
1 T.	olive oil
¼ C.	dry white wine or broth
3 T.	pesto

1. Beat eggs and milk in a small bowl. Pour flour in a flat dish.
2. Preheat oven to 200°F and warm an ovenproof platter.
3. Dust sole with flour, then coat with egg mixture. Set fillets on a cookie rack.
4. Preheat a skillet to medium high heat, add butter and oil. Sauté sole about 2 minutes per side.
5. Transfer sole to warmed oven platter.
6. Pour wine in skillet, loosening little bits on bottom with spoon.
7. Bring wine to a simmer and add pesto, blending sauce quickly.
8. Remove fish from oven, pour sauce over it and serve immediately.

Substitutions: tilapia, catfish, pollock

Tip: Using a cookie rack to "air out" the fish will result in a browner, crisper outer crust.

Nutrients Per Serving:

Calories	311
Omega-3s	494mg
Total Fat	13g
Saturated Fat	4g
Protein	35g
Total Carbohydrate	9g
Cholesterol	170mg
Sodium	206mg
Fiber	1g

Seared Tuna with Asian Cucumber Salad

Yellowfin tuna or ahi, is delicious seared.
Sear cooking requires very high heat.

Prep Time	Cook Time	Yields
5 minutes	1 minute	4 servings

4	4-oz. tuna fillets, at least ½-inch thick
1 T.	oil
1 T.	seafood rub (see page 218)

Cucumber Salad

1	English cucumber, peeled, seeded, thinly sliced
2 T.	red bell pepper, thinly sliced
2 T.	sweet onion, thinly sliced
2 T.	Thai chili sauce
2 T.	rice wine vinegar
¼ tsp.	sugar

Wasabi Sauce

2 T.	wasabi
2 T.	water
1 T.	soy sauce
½ tsp.	powdered ginger

1. Pat fish dry with a paper towel. Coat tuna with seafood rub.
2. Mix cucumber salad. Refrigerate.
3. Mix wasabi sauce in a small bowl. Set aside.
4. Heat oil in a very hot pan.
5. Sear tuna briefly on each side (1 minute or to 80°F. internal temperature). Thinly slice tuna into 8-10 pieces.
6. Lay tuna on serving plate and garnish with cucumber salad.
7. Drizzle wasabi sauce over tuna.

Substitutions: swordfish, marlin, shark

Nutrients Per Serving:

Calories	244
Omega-3's	406mg
Total Fat	11g
Saturated Fat	2g
Protein	11 g
Total Carbohydrates	7g
Cholesterol	43mg
Sodium	199mg
Fiber	1g

Sesame-Soy Mahi-Mahi with Ginger

Mahi-mahi is also called dolphin fish, or dorado.

Prep Time	Cook Time	Yields
5-10 minutes	10-15 minutes	4 servings

1 lb.   mahi-mahi fillets, in 4 pieces

Marinade

2	green onions, thinly sliced
1	garlic clove, minced
1 T.	fresh ginger root, minced
1 T.	soy sauce
1 T.	water
2 tsp.	sesame oil
½ tsp.	black pepper

Tip: *Great on the grill.*

1. Preheat oven to 450°F.
2. Combine all marinade ingredients in a small bowl.
3. Use a large rectangle of foil for each fillet. Pull up sides to form a rectangular packet.
4. Lay one fish fillet in each packet.
5. Evenly divide marinade between packets, turn fish to coat well.
6. Bring foil together on top of fillet, fold. Double-fold two long ends of foil together. Seal tightly. Place on cookie sheet.
7. Bake packets for about 12-15 minutes, or until fish reaches internal temperature of 145° F. Be careful of hot steam when opening packets.
8. Serve with brown rice and stir-fried vegetables.

Substitutions: salmon, grouper, snapper

Nutrients Per Serving:

Calories	124
Omega-3s	137mg
Total Fat	3g
Saturated Fat	1g
Protein	22g
Total Carbohydrate	2g
Cholesterol	83mg
Sodium	359mg
Fiber	1g

Smoked Salmon Omelette

Prep Time	Cook Time	Yields
5-10 minutes	under 5 minutes	1 serving

2 T.   smoked salmon, flaked or diced meat
2   large eggs (1 whole, 1 egg white)
2 T.   fresh parsley, chopped
1 tsp. cold water
salt and pepper to taste
1 T.   light cream cheese
vegetable oil

1. Whisk eggs, parsley, water, salt, pepper in a small bowl.
2. Heat frying pan well-coated with vegetable oil spray on low heat. Pour eggs into pan.
3. Immediately swirl pan to distribute egg mixture evenly on bottom of pan.
4. Sprinkle on salmon and cheese.
5. Cook on medium heat until omelette is set.
6. When eggs are set, quickly remove from heat.
7. Flip over using a fork (or by simply jostling the pan if you can) and serve.

Tip: *To make several omelettes, cook in assembly line fashion.*

Optional Additions: diced sweet onion, tomatoes, red bell peppers, capers.

Substitutions: Smoked trout, whitefish, or other canned or cooked salmon, crab, shrimp.

Nutrients Per Serving:

Calories	219
Omega-3s	331mg
Total Fat	13g
Saturated Fat	4g
Protein	23g
Total Carbohydrate	2g
Cholesterol	436mg
Sodium	706mg
Fiber	1g

Tarragon Cod in Parchment

This is a fun dinner to serve guests. It's easy, impressive and very tasty.

Prep Time	Cook Time	Yields
5-10 minutes	10-15 minutes	4 servings

1 lb.	cod fillet, boneless, skinless, cut into portions
	salt and pepper, to taste
1 C.	mushrooms, sliced
1	medium zucchini, thinly sliced
2 T.	dried tarragon
4 T.	olive oil
4 tsp.	fresh lemon juice

1. Preheat oven to 425° F.
2. Cut four sheets of parchment paper big enough to fold over fish and vegetables.
3. Place 1 cod portion at end of parchment, leaving about 2 inches of paper for sealing parchment.
4. Season cod with salt and pepper. Lay one fourth of sliced mushrooms and zucchini over cod. Sprinkle with one fourth tarragon, olive oil and lemon juice.
5. To close parchment, moisten edges of paper with water. Fold edges of parchment paper over fish, closing like a book. Crimp edges of paper, tightly folding around fish. Assemble 3 more packets.
6. Place packets on a cookie sheet and bake 10 minutes.
7. Place a packet on dinner plate and instruct guests to cut open packets at table. Remove empty packets before digging in.

Substitutions: tilapia, trout, mahi-mahi

Tip: Mix and match vegetables and herbs to whatever is in season or on sale. Serve with wild rice, fresh raspberries and sherbet.

Nutrients Per Serving:

Calories	263
Omega-3s	678mg
Total Fat	4g
Saturated Fat	5g
Protein	32g
Total Carbohydrate	5g
Cholesterol	70mg
Sodium	208mg
Fiber	1g

Teriyaki Salmon with Mango Salsa

Prep Time	Cook Time	Yields
15-20 minutes	5-10 minutes	4 servings

4   6 oz. salmon fillets

Marinade

2 T.   brown sugar, light or dark
2 T.   dry sherry, mirin or sake
2 T.   honey
2 T.   orange juice
2 T.   lemon juice
1 T.   fresh ginger root, finely minced
1 T.   soy sauce
1 tsp.   sesame oil
¼ tsp.   crushed red pepper flakes

Mango Salsa - see the recipe on page 232.

1. Mix all ingredients for salsa. Refrigerate.
2. Mix marinade in a microwavable dish. Microwave for 30 seconds or until sugar dissolves. Stir.
3. Place salmon fillets in dish.
4. Pour marinade over salmon, coating both sides. Cover with microwave proof plastic wrap. Refrigerate for 30 minutes.
5. Turn corner of wrap back to allow steam to escape. Microwave on high for 3 minutes.
6. Rotate dish. Cook until internal temperature reaches 145°F. at thickest part.
7. Top fish with salsa.

Substitutions: yellowfin tuna, trout, grouper

Tip: *Bake fillets in a greased baking dish for 10-12 minutes at 400°F. instead of microwaving.*

Nutrients Per Serving:

Calories	401
Omega-3s	1,812mg
Total Fat	15g
Saturated Fat	3g
Protein	32g
Total Carbohydrate	35g
Cholesterol	88mg
Sodium	485mg
Fiber	2g

Thai-Style Cod
in Packets

Prep Time	Cook Time	Yields
5-10 minutes	20-25 minutes	4 servings

1 lb.	cod fillets, cut in 4 pieces
1	sweet potato, peeled, sliced
1	onion, thinly sliced
2	carrots, sliced lengthwise
½ C.	cilantro, chopped

Marinade

1	14 oz. can low-fat coconut milk
2	green onions, sliced
1	garlic clove, minced
1 T.	fresh ginger root, minced
2 tsp.	fresh cilantro, chopped
2 tsp.	fresh basil, chopped
2 tsp.	lime zest, finely grated
½ tsp.	salt
¼ tsp.	crushed red pepper flakes
¼ tsp.	turmeric

Tip: *Bake all ingredients in a covered, ovenproof dish.*

1. Mix marinade ingredients in a small bowl.
2. Preheat oven to 450°F.
3. Make an aluminum foil packet for each fish fillet. Pull sides up to form a packet.
4. Evenly divide vegetables between packets, top with fish fillets.
5. Pour ¼ of marinade over top of each fillet.
6. Fold foil ends together, sealing tightly. Leave room inside packet for plenty of steam.
7. Place packets on cookie sheet. Bake for 20 minutes.
8. Open cooked packets carefully and garnish with cilantro.

Substitutions: salmon, mahi-mahi, halibut

Nutrients Per Serving:

Calories	214
Omega-3s	217mg
Total Fat	9g
Saturated Fat	7g
Protein	23g
Total Carbohydrate	13g
Cholesterol	49mg
Sodium	383mg
Fiber	3g

Tilapia Pecorino Romano

Pecorino Romano is made from sheep milk under strict guidelines. The sheep are raised naturally, eating wild grass as they have for centuries. Therefore, the cheese contains ALA omega-3s.

Prep Time	Cook Time	Yields
5-10 minutes	10-15 minutes	4 servings

1 lb.	tilapia fillets
2 T.	olive oil
½ C.	fine, dry breadcrumbs
1 T.	fresh parsley, chopped
1 tsp.	garlic powder
½ tsp.	black pepper
¼ tsp.	ground ginger
1	Roma tomato, diced
1 T.	fresh parsley, finely chopped
3 T.	Pecorino Romano cheese, grated

1. Mix breadcrumbs, parsley, garlic powder, pepper, ginger on a plate.
2. Rinse and pat fish dry with a paper towel.
3. Coat fish in crumb mixture.
4. Heat sauté pan with olive oil on medium-high.
5. Pan-fry fish for 4 minutes on each side, or until internal temperature reaches 145°F.
6. Top with tomato, parsley and cheese.

Tip: *Make your own breadcrumbs, which is much cheaper than buying them. Dry out slices of bread, either by oven drying at 200°F. or by setting out on counter overnight. Put in food processor and chop until fine. Can be frozen for future recipes.*

4 slices bread = 1 cup fine dry breadcrumbs

Substitutions: sole, haddock, pollock

Nutrients Per Serving:

Calories	287
Omega-3s	80mg
Total Fat	15g
Saturated Fat	3g
Protein	25g
Total Carbohydrate	12g
Cholesterol	72mg
Sodium	203mg
Fiber	1g

Tuna Noodle Casserole

Prep Time	Cook Time	Yields
5-10 minutes	20 minutes	4 servings

1	6 oz. can albacore tuna, drained, flaked
8 oz.	penne or ziti pasta (tube shapes)
1	10.75 oz. can condensed reduced fat cream of mushroom soup
1 tsp.	dried herbs, such as oregano, thyme, basil
½ tsp.	EACH salt, black ground pepper
vegetable oil cooking spray	
¼ C.	dry breadcrumbs
1 T.	butter, melted

1. Preheat oven to 450°F.
2. Boil pasta until tender but still firm, 10 minutes. Drain well.
3. Mix pasta, tuna, mushroom soup, herbs, pepper and salt in a bowl.
4. Coat 1½-quart casserole with vegetable oil cooking spray. Pour tuna mixture into casserole dish.
5. Top with breadcrumbs and drizzle with butter.
6. Bake uncovered for 20 minutes, until casserole is hot and crumbs are golden brown.

Optional additions

4 oz. mushrooms, sliced
2 Roma tomatoes, chopped
½ C. cheese, grated
2 T. fresh parsley, chopped
1 red bell pepper, diced
½ onion, chopped

Nutrients Per Serving:

Calories	314
Omega-3s	323mg
Total Fat	11g
Saturated Fat	4g
Protein	14g
Total Carbohydrate	39g
Cholesterol	18mg
Sodium	874mg
Fiber	2g

Wine Poached Sockeye Salmon

Sockeye (Red) is a wonderful salmon species to poach. The meat texture is very firm and retains the beautiful red color after cooking.

Prep Time	Cook Time	Yields
5-10 minutes	15-20 minutes	6 servings

2 lbs.	salmon, boneless, skinless, cut into 6 servings
½ C.	dry white wine
¼ C.	fresh lemon juice
water	for poaching
2	shallots, sliced
1	carrot, peeled and cut into 1-inch slices
1	celery stalk, cut into 1-inch slices
2	sprigs fresh parsley, chopped
1	bay leaf
1 tsp.	salt
½ C.	accompaniment, such as Herb Butter, Mango Chutney, or low-fat sour cream, (optional)

Tip: *Make poaching liquid out of chicken broth, milk, apple juice or champagne.*

1. Combine all ingredients except salmon in a deep 12-inch wide pan or skillet. Add enough cold water so it is 2-inches deep.
2. Bring to boil over medium-high heat; reduce heat to simmer and place fillets in pan. Liquid should cover fillet by at least 1-inch; add more water if necessary.
3. Cover and simmer for 10 minutes or until fish reaches 145°F. internal temperature.
4. Serve over brown rice, with your sauce of choice, if desired.

Nutrients Per Serving:

Calories	282
Omega-3s	1,912mg
Total Fat	13g
Saturated Fat	2g
Protein	33g
Total Carbohydrate	4g
Cholesterol	94mg
Sodium	468mg
Fiber	1g

Substitutions: halibut, tuna, sturgeon

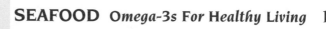

Monkfish Nuggets

Kid-tested. Excellent finger-food

Prep Time	Cook Time	Yields
5 minutes	4 minutes	4 servings

1 lb.	monkfish, boneless, skinless
½ tsp.	lemon-pepper seasoning
1 C.	Ritz Crackers, crushed
2 tsp.	canola oil

1. Cut fish into 2-inch wide nuggets. Pat monkfish dry with paper towel.
2. Pre heat oven to 550° F.
3. Sprinkle fish with lemon-pepper seasoning. Place bread crumbs onto a plate. Roll and press fish in crumbs. Place fish on oiled cookie sheet. Drizzle oil over nuggets.
4. Cook nuggets for about 2 minutes per side until thickest piece of internal temperature reaches 145°F.

Substitutions: shrimp, salmon, mahi-mahi.

Nutrients Per Serving:

Calories	207
Omega-3	370mg
Total fat	9g
Saturated Fat	2g
Protein	22g
Total Carbohydrate	39
Cholesterol	84mg
Sodium	211mg
Fiber	1g

Chapter 11

Shellfish Entrees

Baltimore Crab Cakes

Seafood cakes are found all over the world using local fish, shellfish, herbs and spices. Every country has its own favorite. Asians use shrimp, Scandinavians use cod, Alaskans use salmon. My favorite is halibut.

Prep Time	Cook Time	Yields
5-10 minutes	10-15 minutes	6 servings

1 lb.	crab meat
1	egg, beaten
3 T.	green onions, thinly sliced
3 T.	low-fat mayonnaise
2 tsp.	Worcestershire sauce
2 tsp.	Old Bay seasoning
1 tsp.	fresh lemon juice
½ tsp.	dry mustard
¼ tsp.	ground white pepper
¼ C.	fine dry breadcrumbs, unseasoned
2 T.	olive oil
2 T.	butter

1. Mix egg, onions, mayonnaise, Worcestershire sauce, seasonings in a bowl.
2. Gently mix with crab, add breadcrumbs. Try to leave crab pieces intact as much as possible.
3. Refrigerate mixture for 1-2 hours.
4. Heat oven to 200°F. Warm an ovenproof plate.
5. Form crab mixture into about 12 patties, pressing mixture together with your hands.
6. Heat butter and oil in a medium frying pan, until butter just starts to bubble.
7. Fry crab cakes in batches, 2-4 minutes per side, until golden brown, turning heat down if cakes fry too quickly.
8. Place crab cakes on paper towel lined plate in oven to keep warm.

Substitutions: salmon, cod, halibut, clam, shrimp or scallop meat

Nutrients Per Serving:

Calories	212
Omega-3s	432mg
Total Fat	14g
Saturated Fat	4g
Protein	17g
Total Carbohydrate	5g
Cholesterol	124mg
Sodium	580mg
Fiber	1g

Sweet & Savory Broiled Shrimp

This is quick, easy and very impressive.

Prep Time	Cook Time	Yields
5-10 minutes	5-10 minutes	4 servings

1 lb.	large, raw shrimp, peeled, deveined
1	green bell pepper, cut into 1-inch pieces
1	red onion, cut into 1-inch pieces
1	7.5 oz. can pineapple chunks, drained
¼ C.	Yoshida's Original Gourmet Sweet & Savory sauce
¼ C.	parsley, chopped

1. Mix pepper, onion, pineapple and Yoshida's sauce in a microwave proof bowl, toss to coat evenly. Cover. Marinate in refrigerator for at least 1 hour.
2. Microwave vegetables for 3 minutes.
3. Preheat broiler.
4. Lay foil over broiling pan. Pull up sides of foil to make a tray to contain sauce. Spread on broiler pan in a single layer, shrimp and vegetables.
5. Broil shrimp and vegetables for 2 minutes, turn, broil 2 minutes.
6. Garnish with parsley.

Substitutions: scallops, halibut cheeks

Tip: *To save time, I use store bought sauces and add to it to make a "homemade" flavor. Jazz up this sauce with fresh grated ginger, red pepper flakes, minced garlic and fresh herbs. Serve with steamed rice.*

Nutrients Per Serving:

Calories	152
Omega-3s	581mg
Total Fat	2g
Saturated Fat	1g
Protein	25g
Total Carbohydrate	8g
Cholesterol	172mg
Sodium	860mg

Broiled Shrimp and Vegetables in Lemon Sauce

There are a lot of choices in purchasing shrimp: with tail, head, shell on or off; vein in or out; cooked or raw. Shrimp are graded by numbers of shrimp per pound, called count.

   100 to 500 count-cooked, tiny: used for salads
   50 to 70 count, small: used for party appetizers, skewers
   31 to 40 count, large: great size to butterfly cut or sauté
   21 to under 11 count, jumbo: impressive & expensive

Prep Time	Cook Time	Yields
5-10 minutes	5 minutes	4 servings

1½ lb.	raw large shrimp, peeled, deveined
1 C.	mushrooms, thinly sliced
1	zucchini, thinly sliced
1	red onion, thinly sliced

Lemon Sauce

2 T.	fresh lemon juice
1 T.	olive oil
1	garlic clove, minced
1 tsp.	dried oregano
½ tsp.	salt
¼ tsp.	pepper

1. Preheat oven to broil.
2. Mix lemon juice, oil, garlic, seasonings in a bowl.
3. Place shrimp and vegetables in a single layer in a baking dish. Pour sauce evenly over shrimp and vegetables.
4. Broil 5 inches from heat source for 3 minutes. Turn and broil for 2 minutes.

Substitutions: scallops, salmon chunks, oyster meat

Nutrients Per Serving:

Calories	383
Omega-3s	643mg
Total Fat	6g
Saturated Fat	1g
Protein	35g
Total Carbohydrate	46g
Cholesterol	174mg
Sodium	836mg
Fiber	3g

Cashew Broccoli Shrimp Stir-fry

Shrimp are low-fat so watch cooking time very carefully.

Prep Time	Cook Time	Yields
5-10 minutes	5-10 minutes	4 servings

1 lb.	raw large shrimp, peeled, deveined
3 C.	broccoli florets
2	garlic cloves, minced
2 tsp.	fresh ginger root, minced
canola oil	
3	green onions, sliced
3 T.	cashew halves

Sauce

2 T.	hoisin or soy sauce
1 T.	sesame oil
½ tsp.	crushed red pepper flakes

1. Combine soy sauce, sesame oil, crushed red pepper flakes in small bowl. Set aside.
2. Preheat a large skillet on medium-high heat.
3. Add oil, garlic, ginger, shrimp. Sauté 2 minutes. Remove from pan. Add broccoli and cook for 5 minutes.
4. Return shrimp to pan, add green onions and sauce.
5. Cook for 2 minutes, stirring constantly.
6. Stir in cashews and serve.

Enjoy tasty and moist shrimp using this cooking guide:
Jumbo Shrimp: 3½-4 minutes
Large Shrimp: 2½-3 minutes
Small Shrimp: 1½-2 minutes

Nutrients Per Serving:

Calories	212
Omega-3s	600mg
Total Fat	6g
Saturated Fat	1g
Protein	27g
Total Carbohydrate	13g
Cholesterol	173mg
Sodium	323mg
Fiber	2g

Garlic Wine Mussels

This classic recipe put mussels on the American dinner table. I used it for years, teaching on my TV show, at cooking demonstrations and in seminars across the country.

Prep Time	Cook Time	Yields
10 minutes	10 minutes	4 servings

4 lb.	mussels, in shell, scrubbed
2 T.	butter
2	shallots, chopped
3	garlic cloves, minced
1	small leek, finely chopped
1	lemon, juice and zest, separated
1 T.	fresh thyme, minced, or 1 tsp. dried thyme
1 C.	dry white wine or broth
½ C.	Italian parsley, chopped

1. Melt butter in a large saucepan over medium heat.
2. Sauté shallots, garlic, leek, lemon juice, zest, thyme, for 3 minutes. Add mussels and pour in wine. Cover.
3. Cook mussels for 3-6 minutes, until all open, shaking pan frequently (but without removing the lid). Discard any mussels that don't open.
4. Garnish with parsley.
5. Serve with thick, coarse bread for dipping in wine sauce.

Substitutions: clams, cockles in shell

Tip: *Use empty mussel shell as a tweezer to extract meat from shells.*

Nutrients Per Serving:

Calories	319
Omega-3s	413mg
Total Fat	11g
Saturated Fat	4g
Protein	28g
Total Carbohydrate	16g
Cholesterol	80mg
Sodium	705mg
Fiber	1g

Greek Shrimp with Tomatoes and Feta Cheese

Prep Time	Cook Time	Yields
10-15 minutes	10-15 minutes	4 servings

1 lb.	raw shrimp, peeled, deveined
1 T.	olive oil
2	shallots, sliced
2	garlic cloves, minced
1	14.5 oz. can crushed tomatoes, undrained
½ C.	dry white wine or broth
2 T.	fresh mint, minced
1 T.	dried oregano, crumbled
½ tsp.	crushed red pepper flakes
¼ tsp.	salt
½ C.	feta cheese, coarsely crumbled
¼ C.	parsley, chopped

Tip: *Serve over pasta or rice with spinach salad and fruit.*

1. Heat oil in a large frying pan. Sauté shallots and garlic about 1 minute. Add tomatoes, wine, mint, oregano, red pepper flakes, salt.
2. Boil uncovered for 5 minutes. Stir often to reduce liquid.
3. Stir in shrimp.
4. Reduce heat to low, cook about 3 minutes.
5. Garnish with cheese and parsley.

Substitutions: calico or bay scallops

Nutrients Per Serving:

Calories	269
Omega-3s	399mg
Total Fat	8g
Saturated Fat	3g
Protein	34g
Total Carbohydrate	11g
Cholesterol	241mg
Sodium	495mg
Fiber	2g

Shrimp and Asparagus

Prep Time	Cook Time	Yields
10-15 minutes	5-10 minutes	4 servings

1 lb.	large, raw shrimp, peeled, deveined
1 T.	soy sauce
1 tsp.	sesame oil
2 T.	canola oil
2	garlic cloves, minced
1 T.	fresh ginger root, minced
1 lb.	asparagus, trimmed and cut into 2-inch pieces
1	green onion, sliced
2 T.	mirin
1 T.	sesame seeds

1. Toss shrimp with soy sauce and sesame oil in a bowl.
2. Heat canola oil in a large pan on high until hot (nearly smoking). Add shrimp, garlic, ginger.
3. Cook over medium-high heat, stirring about 3 minutes. Remove from pan.
4. Cook asparagus in pan until bright green, about 1 minute. Add green onion and mirin.
5. Return shrimp to pan and heat about 1 minute longer. Sprinkle with sesame seeds.

Substitutions: sea scallop, steak fish strips

Tip: *Mirin is a sweet rice seasoning. It's quite often the secret ingredient to authentic Japanese cuisine. Sushi rice vinegar can be substituted.*

Nutrients Per Serving:

Calories	241
Omega-3s	399mg
Total Fat	10g
Saturated Fat	1g
Protein	26g
Total Carbohydrate	12g
Cholesterol	172mg
Sodium	437mg
Fiber	3g

Microwave Shrimp (Prawns)

The words shrimp and prawns are used interchangeably as a marketing term to "elevate" shrimp to a more expensive level.

Prep Time	Cook Time	Yields
5-10 minutes	2-3 minutes	4 servings

1 lb.	raw jumbo shrimp (prawns) peeled, deveined
2 T.	olive oil
⅓ C.	white wine
1 T.	lemon-pepper seasoning
1 tsp.	Italian seasoning
¼ tsp.	cayenne pepper

fresh parsley, to garnish

1. Mix all ingredients except shrimp in 2-quart microwaveable dish.
2. Microwave, covered, on high for 30 seconds to blend ingredients.
3. In one layer, arrange shrimp on dish. Cover. Microwave on high for 1-2 minutes.
4. Garnish with fresh parsley.

Substitutions: sole, haddock, tilapia

Tip: *Arrange shrimp or fish in a microwave dish with the thickest parts pointing outward and the thinner parts toward the center of the dish. Tuck the thin tail section underneath the fillet for more even cooking.*

Nutrients Per Serving:

Calories	339
Omega-3	349mg
Total Fat	12g
Saturated Fat	4g
Protein	35g
Total Carbohydrate	16g
Cholesterol	89mg
Sodium	230mg
Fiber	1g

Mussels and Italian Sausage Marinara

Did you know that mussels contain 32% of your daily iron needs?

Prep Time	Cook Time	Yields
5-10 minutes	5-10 minutes	6 servings

5 lbs.	mussels, in shell, cleaned, scrubbed
2 tsp.	olive oil
½ lb.	low-fat chicken or turkey Italian sausage
1/2 C.	Italian parsley, chopped
2 tsp.	garlic, minced
½ tsp.	red pepper flakes, crushed
1	14.5 oz. can low-sodium Italian tomatoes, chopped, undrained
1 C.	white wine or broth

1. Heat a very large skillet that has a tight-fitting lid.
2. Add oil and sliced or crumbled sausage. Sauté until lightly browned.
3. Add mussels, parsley, garlic, red pepper flakes, tomatoes and wine. Stir to blend ingredients.
4. Cover and cook until all mussels are open, 3-6 minutes. Discard any that don't open.

Nutrients Per Serving:

Calories	165
Omega-3	339mg
Total Fat	12g
Saturated Fat	5g
Protein	20g
Total Carbohydrate	0g
Cholesterol	180mg
Sodium	635mg
Fiber	1g

Normandy Steamed Mussels

We ate our way through France enjoying mussels fixed many ways.

Prep Time	Cook Time	Yields
5-10 minutes	5-10 minutes	4 servings

4 lbs.   mussels, in shell, cleaned, debearded
2 C.   heavy cream
½   orange, juice, grated rind
½ C.   parsley, chopped
1 C.   green onion, sliced
salt, to taste

Tip: *The fat content of heavy cream will prevent it from curdling and separating when it is heated slowly. Do not substitute with light cream.*

1. Scrub mussels in cold water, just before cooking.
2. Mix cream, orange juice and rind, parsley, green onion in a large pot.
3. Add mussels, stir and cover. Cook on medium heat. Add salt to taste.
4. Check after 5 minutes and stir; continue cooking until shells open. Discard any that remain closed.

Nutrients Per Serving:

Calories	435
Omega-3s	566mg
Total Fat	9g
Saturated Fat	3g
Protein	28g
Total Carbohydrate	10g
Cholesterol	64mg
Sodium	471mg
Fiber	1g

Pan-Fried Oysters with Tartar Caper Sauce

Prep Time	Cook Time	Yields
5-10 minutes	10-15 minutes	4 servings

24	oysters, extra-small, shucked
¾ C.	flour
½ tsp.	EACH salt, black pepper, cayenne, dillweed, garlic powder, ginger
½ C.	canola oil

Caper Sauce

1 C.	plain low-fat yogurt, drained
2 T.	light mayonnaise
2 T.	capers, rinsed
1 T.	parsley, chopped
1 T.	green onion, chopped
dash	hot sauce

1. Mix sauce ingredients in a bowl. Refrigerate several hours or overnight.
2. Mix flour, seasoning in a shallow container.
3. Coat oysters in flour mixture. Set aside.
4. Heat oil in a frying pan on medium-high.
5. Fry oysters in batches, 2 minutes per side or until nicely browned. Drain on paper towels.
6. Serve oysters with caper sauce.

Substitutions: scallops, halibut cheeks, salmon nuggets

Tip: *Boil oysters in water for 1 minute. This will make the meat more firm. Thoroughly dry.*

Nutrients Per Serving:

Calories	385
Omega-3s	700mg
Total Fat	12g
Saturated Fat	2g
Protein	18g
Total Carbohydrate	40g
Cholesterol	117mg
Sodium	699mg
Fiber	1g

Scallop Stir-Fry with Snow Peas

Scallops are sold by size and the biggest ones cost the most. Sea scallops: 9-12 per pound. Bay scallops: 50-90 per pound. Calico scallops: 70-200 per pound.

Prep Time	Cook Time	Yields
35 minutes	5-10 minutes	4 servings

1 ½ lb. bay scallops

Marinade

3 T.	rice vinegar
2 T.	low-sodium soy sauce
¾ C.	chicken broth
1 tsp.	ginger powder
½ tsp.	red pepper flakes
2 tsp.	cornstarch

3 T.	olive oil
¼ lb.	snow peas, vertically sliced
2	green onions, thinly sliced
1	red bell pepper, thinly sliced
1	celery stalk, thinly sliced
1	8 oz. can sliced water chestnuts, drained

Salt and pepper, to taste

1. Mix marinade in a self-sealing plastic bag. Add scallops, turning to coat. Refrigerate. Marinate for 20 minutes.
2. Heat 2 T. of olive oil on high in a wok or large skillet. Add vegetables.
3. Stir-fry over high heat for about 4 minutes, until vegetables begin to soften. Remove from wok and place on a serving platter.
4. Heat remaining olive oil in skillet.
5. Remove scallops from marinade. Reserve marinade. Stir-fry 2-3 minutes.
6. Return vegetables to skillet.
7. Pour marinade over vegetables and scallops.
8. Cook on medium-high, stirring constantly, until slightly thickened, 1-5 minutes.
9. Season with salt and pepper.

Tip: *Stir-fry cooking looks complicated but it isn't. You can save time when you buy pre-cut bagged vegetables or supermarket salad bar vegetables.*

Nutrients Per Serving:

Calories	297
Omega-3s	366mg
Total Fat	12g
Saturated Fat	2g
Protein	31g
Total Carbohydrate	17g
Cholesterol	56mg
Sodium	590mg
Fiber	3g

Shrimp Enchiladas

Seafood enchiladas may sound a bit risky but, trust me, it's one of our favorites.

Prep Time	Cook Time	Yields
10 minutes	30 minutes	8 servings

1 lb.	cooked salad shrimp
8	12-inch whole wheat flour tortillas
2 C.	pepper Jack cheese, grated,
1	4 oz. can green chilies, diced, drained
1 C.	low-fat sour cream
1 can	reduced fat cream of chicken condensed soup
1 C.	chunky thick salsa, drained thoroughly

1. Preheat oven to 375°F.
2. Mix shrimp, 1½ C. cheese and chilies, in a bowl. Lay tortilla flat on your working surface. Fill each tortilla with ⅛ of mixture. Roll up tortilla.
3. Spread sour cream on bottom of pan. Place rolled tortillas, single file, seam-side-down in a 9x12-inch baking dish.
4. Blend soup and salsa in a small bowl, evenly coat enchiladas. Sprinkle with remaining cheese.
5. Bake for 30 minutes or until cheese is melted and bubbly.

Substitutions: cooked salmon, lobster or crab meat

Tip: *Heat tortillas slightly in the microwave before you fill them. This will make them more pliable so they won't split during the cooking process.*

Nutrients Per Serving:

Calories	410
Omega-3s	371mg
Total Fat	12g
Saturated Fat	5g
Protein	26g
Total Carbohydrate	51g
Cholesterol	130mg
Sodium	930mg
Fiber	3g

Parsley Stuffed Green-Lipped Mussels

This mussel, unique to New Zealand, is thought to help inflammation, stiffness and pain. See Loyola University Health Systems at www.luhs.org for more information.

Prep Time	Cook Time	Yields
5 minutes	10 minutes	4 servings

16   green-lipped mussels in half shell

Stuffing
1 T.   olive oil
6   garlic cloves, minced
1 C.   white wine or broth
2 T.   butter
½ C.   fresh parsley, chopped
salt and pepper, to taste
1 C.   seasoned bread crumbs

1. Preheat oven to 450°F.
2. Heat oil over medium heat in a pan. Sauté garlic for 30 seconds. Add white wine and boil until wine is reduced by half. Add butter and parsley. Season. Stir.
3. Crumple sheet of aluminum foil, place on cookie sheet. Lay mussel shells, meat side up securely in foil to prevent sauce from spilling out. Spread stuffing over each mussel. Top with crumbs.
4. Bake for 10 minutes.

Substitutions: oysters, lobster or crab legs in shell

Nutrients Per Serving:

Calories	337
Omega-3s	430mg
Total Fat	12g
Saturated Fat	4g
Protein	35g
Total Carbohydrate	10g
Cholesterol	120mg
Sodium	205mg
Fiber	1g

Stuffed Calamari (Squid)

Squid fishing is fun. They migrate into Puget Sound from the Pacific coast in the cold, rainy, winter months. All you need to catch them is a pole, squid jig and a good jerk! Jerking the jig up and down in the water attracts them to your pole. When they strike the jig, pull them up. Look out! They will spray you with their highly prized squid ink as you reel them aboard.

Prep Time	**Cook Time**	**Yields**
10-15 minutes	50-60 minutes	4 servings

1 lb.	squid, tubes
½ C.	white wine or broth
2 T.	olive oil
3 T.	fresh parsley, minced

Stuffing

1. Preheat oven to 450°F.
2. Prepare one of the stuffing recipes below.
3. Fill each squid with 1 to 2 T. of stuffing. Close squid tube by securing it with a toothpick. Lay inside ovenproof pan in a single layer.
4. Add white wine, olive oil, parsley, enough water to just cover squid. Cover pan.
5. Bake squid 45 minutes, or until tender.

STUFFING OPTIONS

Italian Tomato

1 C.	fresh tomatoes, diced
½ C.	onion, chopped
1 tsp.	olive oil
¼ tsp.	dried oregano
¼ tsp.	dried rosemary, crushed

1. Sauté ingredients in a pan in oil over medium heat until translucent.

recipe continued ☞

-Recipe continued-

Broccoli-Parmesan

1 C.   broccoli, coarsely chopped
¼ C.   Parmesan cheese, grated

1. In microwave or in a saucepan, steam broccoli in a few tablespoons of water until bright green, but not mushy.
2. Drain. Stir in Parmesan cheese.

Cilantro Lime Salsa

1   small jalapeño, seeded, diced
1   Anaheim pepper, seeded, diced
½ C.   onion, chopped
½ C.   tomato, chopped
¼ C.   fresh cilantro, chopped
2 T.   fresh lime juice

1. Mix all ingredients in a medium bowl.
2. If possible, refrigerate for 1 hour to allow flavors to blend.

Prosciutto and Mushroom

1   garlic clove, minced
1 T.   butter
½ C.   prosciutto, coarsely chopped
½ C.   mushrooms, coarsely chopped
Dash   nutmeg

1. Sauté garlic and mushrooms in butter for 5 minutes.
2. Add prosciutto and nutmeg; cook 1 minute longer.

Nutrients Per Serving:

Calories	250
Omega-3s	425mg
Total Fat	5g
Saturated Fat	1g
Protein	15g
Total Carbohydrate	2g
Cholesterol	220mg
Sodium	470mg
Fiber	1g

Tandoori-Style Prawns

Prep Time	Cook Time	Yields
5 minutes	10 minutes	4 servings

1 lb.   large prawns, peeled, deveined
½ C.   plain, low-fat yogurt
1 tsp.   fresh lime juice
½ tsp.   turmeric
¼ tsp.   ground cumin
¼ tsp.   cayenne pepper
¼ tsp.   salt
Lime wedges, to serve

1. Preheat oven to 450°F.
2. Stir yogurt, lime juice, seasonings in a bowl. Toss with prawns to coat.
3. Place prawns on cookie sheet in a single layer. Pour remaining sauce over prawns. Bake for 3 minutes.
4. Turn prawns and bake until prawns are pink, about 3 more minutes.

Substitutions: tuna, swordfish, orange roughy

Nutrients Per Serving:

Calories	198
Omega-3s	399mg
Total Fat	3g
Saturated Fat	1g
Protein	27g
Total Carbohydrate	4g
Cholesterol	173mg
Sodium	323mg
Fiber	0

Chapter 12

Grilling

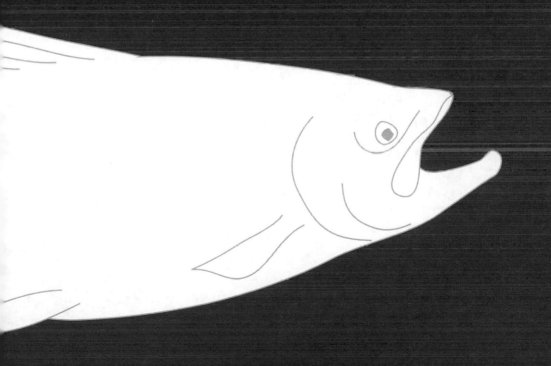

Cedar Plank Roasted Halibut with Cucumber-Dill Sauce

If you don't have a wood roasting plank, don't worry! This is delicious when roasted in a baking pan.

Prep Time	Cook Time	Yields
5-10 minutes	30-40 minutes	4 servings

1 lb.	halibut, skinless, boneless
	Cedar roasting plank
1	fresh lemon, cut in half
	Salt and pepper, to taste
8-10	low-fat Ritz crackers, crushed
2 T.	butter, melted

1. Preheat oven to 375°F.
2. Cut halibut into 4 serving pieces.
3. Fold aluminum foil into a tray with sides turned up and put on cedar roasting plank.
4. Place halibut inside foil tray leaving space between pieces.
5. Squeeze juice from lemon halves (about 2 T.) onto fish and sprinkle fish with salt and pepper.
6. Mix butter and cracker crumbs and coat top of fish.
7. Roast uncovered 30-40 minutes or until internal temperature of thickest part of fillets reaches 145°F.
8. Remove from plank and serve with sauce.

Tip: *Roast halibut without thawing, taking it directly from the freezer. Just double the cooking time.*

Cucumber-Dill Sauce

½ C.	low-fat sour cream
½ C.	cucumber, grated and squeezed dry
1 T.	fresh dill, chopped
1 T.	fresh lemon juice
1 tsp.	garlic, minced
	Salt and pepper

1. Mix sauce ingredients and refrigerate to blend flavors.
2. Serve with fish.

Nutrients Per Serving:

Calories	201
Omega-3s	480mg
Total Fat	9g
Saturated Fat	3g
Protein	4g
Total Carbohydrate	4g
Cholesterol	52mg
Sodium	224mg
Fiber	1g

Chipotle Keta Salmon

Keta is the last salmon to migrate home after living four years in wild, open ocean. It was given the slang term, "dog salmon" because the Alaska natives dried and fed this salmon to their sled dogs during the long, cold winter. It's highly prized now and can be bought under several marketing names including chum, keta and silverbrite.

Prep Time	**Cook Time**	**Yields**
5-10 minutes	10 minutes	4 servings

1 lb.   chum (keta, silverbrite) salmon, boneless, skinless
vegetable oil cooking spray

Chipotle Sauce
2 T.   canola oil
1   sweet onion, sliced
2 T.   brown sugar
1 tsp.   chipotle in adobo sauce (from a can)
½ tsp.   salt

1. Preheat grill to medium high heat. Coat salmon with vegetable oil cooking spray. Place on grill rack for 4 minutes, turn and cook until internal temperature reaches 145°F.
2. Simmer all sauce ingredients in a pan for 10 minutes, being careful not to burn.
3. Place grilled fish on serving platter. Pour sauce over the salmon.

Substitutions: catfish, grouper, mahi-mahi

Nutrients Per Serving:

Calories	294
Omega-3s	673mg
Total Fat	19g
Saturated Fat	4g
Protein	23g
Total Carbohydrate	8g
Cholesterol	57mg
Sodium	355mg
Fiber	1g

Coconut Shrimp

Prep Time	Cook Time	Yields
5-10 minutes	4-6 minutes	4 servings

1 lb.	raw shrimp, peeled and deveined
1 C.	coconut, flaked
¼ C.	fresh parsley, minced
1 tsp.	salt
¼ tsp.	garlic powder
1 T.	olive oil

1. Soak 12 wooden skewers in water for 30 minutes.
2. Preheat grill to medium high.
3. Mix coconut, parsley, salt and garlic powder on a large plate.
4. Toss shrimp in olive oil and thread on soaked skewers.
5. Press shrimp skewers into plate of the coconut mixture, coating well.
6. Grill for 2-3 minutes per side, until pink.

Substitutions: coconut mixture can be used as a coating for pan-fried sole, pollock and tilapia.

Nutrients Per Serving:

Calories	263
Omega-3s	639mg
Total Fat	7g
Saturated Fat	1g
Protein	27g
Total Carbohydrate	22g
Cholesterol	172mg
Sodium	950mg
Fiber	2g

French Oak Smoked Salmon

The French oak staves from wine soaked barrels add a wonderful smoke flavor to salmon. Set the water-soaked staves on the grill, get them smoking, then add fish. Oak is a very hard wood so it takes awhile to get it to smoke.

Prep Time	Cook Time	Yields
35 minutes	10-20 minutes	6 servings

1½ lb. salmon fillet, cut into serving sized pieces
Salt and pepper, to taste

Marinade
¼ C.   Chardonnay
¼ C.   low-fat chicken broth
3 T.   olive oil
2   garlic cloves, minced
2 T.   fresh parsley, chopped
1 T.   tarragon, dried
¼ tsp salt

1. Combine all marinade ingredients in a dish large enough to marinate salmon fillet.
2. Coat salmon with marinade. Cover. Refrigerate for 30 minutes.
3. Preheat grill to medium-low.
4. Grill slowly for 5 minutes per side, turning once during grilling.

Substitutions: mahi-mahi, bass, grouper

Nutrients Per Serving:

Calories	451
Omega-3s	1400g
Total Fat	9g
Saturated Fat	2g
Protein	24g
Total Carbohydrate	3g
Cholesterol	65mg
Sodium	465mg
Fiber	1g

Garlic Lime Salmon

Prep Time	Cook Time	Yields
35 minutes	10 minutes	6 servings

1½ lb.   salmon fillet, cut into serving sized pieces

Marinade
3 T.   olive oil
2 T.   soy sauce
2 T.   fresh orange juice
1 tsp.   garlic powder
1 tsp.   crushed red pepper flakes
1½ tsp. brown sugar

1. Mix marinade ingredients in a plastic self-sealing bag.
2. Place salmon in bag, seal, refrigerate for 30 minutes.
3. Preheat grill to medium-high.
4. Grill over direct heat for 3 minutes, move salmon over indirect heat and finish grilling for 5 minutes or until internal temperature reaches 145° F.
5. Serve with Cranberry Salsa. (see page 245)

Substitutions: tuna, swordfish, mahi-mahi

Nutrients Per Serving:

Calories	318
Omega-3s	1400mg
Total Fat	5g
Saturated Fat	2g
Protein	24g
Total Carbohydrate	2g
Cholesterol	65mg
Sodium	195mg
Fiber	3g

Grilled Whitefish with Sauerkraut

Prep Time	Cook Time	Yields
5-10 minutes	25-30 minutes	4 servings

1 lb.	whitefish fillet
1 C.	sauerkraut, rinsed, drained
⅓ C.	fresh dill
⅓ C.	low-fat mayonnaise
⅓ C.	low-fat sour cream
1 T.	butter, melted
1 T.	Homemade Old Bay (page 219)
1 T.	Worcestershire sauce
2	garlic cloves, minced
¼ tsp.	cayenne pepper (optional)

1. Preheat grill to medium.
2. Double a piece of foil that is large enough to fit fish, fold up all 4 sides to make a tray.
3. Place fish on tray and top with sauerkraut.
4. Mix remaining ingredients in a bowl and then spread over sauerkraut.
5. Grill in foil tray until internal temperature reaches 145°F. at thickest part.

Substitutions: catfish, bass, haddock

Nutrients Per Serving:

Calories	235
Omega-3s	500mg
Total Fat	11g
Saturated Fat	3g
Protein	26g
Total Carbohydrate	7g
Cholesterol	50mg
Sodium	660mg
Fiber	1g

Grilled Mahi-Mahi with Spicy Asian Glaze

Prep Time	Cook Time	Yields
5-10 minutes	10-15 minutes	4 servings

1 lb.   mahi-mahi fillets
canola oil

Marinade
½ C.   fresh lemon juice
¼ C.   hoisin sauce
2   garlic cloves, minced
2 T.   fresh ginger root, peeled, minced
2 T.   peanut oil
2 T.   light soy sauce
2 T.   rice vinegar
3 dashes chili oil

1. Mix marinade and pour over fish in a shallow dish. Cover. Refrigerate for 30 minutes, turning several times.
2. Preheat a grill to medium high. Grease rack.
3. Reserve marinade. Grill fillets 3 minutes per side, or until internal temperature reaches 145°F.
4. Transfer fish to serving plate.
5. Boil reserved marinade for at least 5 minutes, pour over fish.

Alternative: Broil fish on oiled broiler pan 4 inches from heat.

Substitutions: whitefish, tuna, catfish

Nutrients Per Serving:

Calories	213
Omega-3s	791mg
Total Fat	8g
Saturated Fat	1g
Protein	22g
Total Carbohydrate	12g
Cholesterol	83mg
Sodium	874mg
Fiber	1g

Grilled Tuna with Lemon Caper Sauce

Many chefs cook tuna until the internal temperature of the thickest part of the fish reaches 120°F. or less. Watch the thermometer to decide your personal preference.

Prep Time	Cook Time	Yields
5-10 minutes	10-15 minutes	6 servings

1½ lb. tuna

Lemon Caper Sauce

4 T.	capers, drained, washed
3 T.	fresh lemon juice
3 T.	butter, melted
1 tsp.	dried basil
½ tsp.	salt
¼ tsp.	pepper

Garnish with chopped parsley

Tip: *Just before serving, use a toothpick to poke small holes in cooked tuna to infuse meat with sauce.*

1. Pre-heat grill to medium-hot. Place fish on oiled grill.
2. Grill until internal temperature reaches your personal preference or 145°F. at thickest part.
3. Mix sauce ingredients in microwave proof container. Cook about 30 seconds until just heated. Pour over tuna.
4. Garnish.

Substitutions: striped bass, grouper, salmon

Nutrients Per Serving:

Calories	195
Omega-3s	946mg
Total Fat	11g
Saturated Fat	4g
Protein	23g
Total Carbohydrate	1g
Cholesterol	60mg
Sodium	509mg
Fiber	1g

Grilled Vegetable Stuffed Trout

Place on a soaked hickory grilling plank to add smoky flavor.

Prep Time	Cook Time	Yields
10-15 minutes	20 minutes	4 servings

4   6 oz. whole trout, dressed, cleaned
vegetable oil spray or oil

Stuffing
2   celery stalks, finely chopped
½   onion, finely chopped
1 T.   fresh dill, chopped
1 T.   fresh parsley, chopped
salt, pepper to taste
½   lemon, thinly sliced

1. Mix stuffing ingredients in a medium bowl. Spread evenly into trout body cavity. Place lemon slices in single layer over stuffing.
2. Tie each fish shut in 2-3 places with all-cotton string.
3. Preheat grill to medium heat.
4. Place on grill over indirect heat.
5. Cover grill and slow cook for 20 minutes, or until internal temperature reaches 165°F. at thickest part.

Substitution: one whole pink salmon or tilapia

Nutrients Per Serving:

Calories	217
Omega-3s	1,205mg
Total Fat	6g
Saturated Fat	1g
Protein	35g
Total Carbohydrate	4g
Cholesterol	100mg
Sodium	216mg
Fiber	1g

Lemon-Pepper Salmon Steaks

I like to grill seafood steaks because the skin and bones add more flavor. Buy uniformly thick steaks for even cooking time.

Prep Time	Cook Time	Yields
5-10 minutes	6-10 minutes	4 servings

1½ lb. salmon steaks, 4 pieces
Vegetable oil spray

Marinade
½ C.   white wine or chicken broth
2   garlic cloves, minced
1 T.   olive oil
1 tsp. lemon-pepper seasoning
¼ tsp. salt

1. Mix wine, garlic, oil, seasonings in a small bowl.
2. Spray salmon with oil. Place on preheated, medium-hot grill.
3. Cook salmon for 3-5 minutes on each side, basting with lemon-pepper marinade, until fish reaches internal temperature of 145° F.

Substitutions: black cod, tuna, bluefish

Nutrients Per Serving:

Calories	151
Omega-3s	1100mg
Total Fat	7g
Saturated Fat	2g
Protein	22g
Total Carbohydrate	29g
Cholesterol	83mg
Sodium	249mg
Fiber	3g

Mahi-Mahi
with Pineapple Glaze

Prep Time	Cook Time	Yields
10 minutes	15 minutes	4 servings

1 lb. mahi-mahi, cut in serving-size pieces

Pineapple Glaze

1	garlic clove, minced
2 tsp.	curry powder
⅛ tsp.	allspice
⅛ tsp.	salt and pepper
2 T.	soy sauce
1	10 oz. can pineapple chunks, drained
2 T.	red bell pepper, diced
2 T.	green onion, chopped
2 T.	fresh cilantro, chopped

1. Preheat grill on medium-high. Tear a sheet of heavy-duty aluminum foil a little bigger than fish. Fold up sides and ends of foil to make a tray.
2. Lay fish inside foil tray, leaving space between pieces.
3. Simmer garlic, curry, allspice, salt and pepper, soy sauce and pineapple in saucepan for 5 minutes.
4. Spoon sauce over fish in tray.
5. Place foil tray on grill rack over indirect heat. Slow grill for about 15 minutes or until internal temperature of fish reaches 145° F.
6. Garnish with peppers, green onion and cilantro.

Substitutions: haddock, tuna, swordfish

Tip: *Make individual foil trays and serve directly from grill to table. Microwave a sweet potato. Serve vegetable sticks and dip to make dinner an easy clean-up.*

Nutrient Per Serving:

Calories	218
Omega-3s	416mg
Total Fat	2g
Saturated Fat	1g
Protein	29g
Total Carbohydrate	29g
Cholesterol	83mg
Sodium	249mg
Fiber	3g

Mesquite Smoked Bluefish with Lemon and Thyme

Prep Time	Cook Time	Yields
5-10 minutes	10-15 minutes	6 servings

1 ½ lb.	bluefish fillets
1	Captain H's Grill Smoker, mesquite

¼ C.	dry white wine
salt and pepper, to taste	
½ tsp.	dried thyme, crushed
½ C.	onions, thinly sliced
1	lemon, thinly sliced

1. Preheat grill on high. Place Grill Smoker over hottest part of grill. Turn down heat to medium-high when Grill Smoker starts smoking.
2. Tear a sheet of heavy-duty aluminum foil a little bigger than fish. Fold up sides and ends of foil, about an inch, to make a water-proof tray. Pour wine in foil tray.
3. Place fish on foil. Sprinkle with salt, pepper and thyme.
4. Cover fish with onion slices. Lay lemon slices on top of onions.
5. Place foil tray on cool side of grill rack. Close grill lid.
6. Smoke, cook bluefish until internal temperature reaches 145°F. at thickest part.
7. Serve directly from tray.

Substitutions: striped sea bass, salmon, mackerel

Tip: *Use an alder, hickory or apple Grill Smoker to vary smoke flavor.*

Nutrients Per Serving:

Calories	296
Omega-3s	800mg
Total Fat	4g
Saturated Fat	1g
Protein	20g
Total Carbohydrate	0
Cholesterol	65mg
Sodium	65mg
Fiber	3g

Raspberry-Glazed Catfish

Prep Time	Cook Time	Yields
5-10 minutes	10 minutes	6 servings

1 ½ lbs.   catfish fillets, skinless, boneless
½ C.   raspberry or blackberry jam
½ C.   white wine
¼ C.   parsley, coarsely chopped
1 T.   Dijon mustard
1 ½ C.   fresh raspberries or blackberries

1. Mix jam, wine, parsley, mustard in a gallon zip-lock bag.
2. Add catfish to bag, seal and coat fillets completely.
3. Refrigerate in bag for 4 hours.
4. Leaving as much marinade on fish as you can, grill fish on coolest part of grill until internal temperature reaches 145°F. at thickest part.
5. Garnish fish with berries.

Substitutions: pike, swordfish, orange roughy

Nutrients Per Serving:

Calories	222
Omega-3s	354mg
Total Fat	7g
Saturated Fat	2g
Protein	14g
Total Carbohydrate	22g
Cholesterol	40mg
Sodium	114mg
Fiber	2g

Snapper with Herb-Pecan Crust

Prep Time	Cook Time	Yields
5-10 minutes	about 5 minutes	4 servings

1½ lb. snapper fillets, boneless, skin-on, about ½-inch thick
1 T.   butter, melted
salt and pepper, to taste
lemon wedges, to serve

Crust
½ C.   pecans, ground or finely chopped
2   garlic cloves, minced
2 T.   seasoned dry breadcrumbs
1 T.   fresh parsley, chopped
1 tsp. lemon zest, finely chopped
1 tsp. rosemary, crushed

Tip: *Do not turn fish. Cover grill to infuse more smoke. Use food processor to grind nuts, being careful to not grind too long or you'll have pecan nut butter!*

1. Preheat grill to medium heat.
2. Combine all crust ingredients in a small bowl.
3. Pat fish very dry with paper towel.
4. Spread each fillet thinly with butter, season lightly with salt and pepper.
5. Spoon crust mixture over each fillet and press in gently on top.
6. Grill over medium heat, on greased rack, for about 4-6 minutes, or until internal temperature reaches 145° F.

Substitutions: salmon, halibut, haddock

Nutrients Per Serving:

Calories	280
Omega-3s	585mg
Total Fat	15g
Saturated Fat	3g
Protein	31g
Total Carbohydrate	25g
Cholesterol	61mg
Sodium	358mg
Fiber	2g

Scallops in Thai-Style Peanut Sauce

Scallops are sold either dry or wet. Dry means they are just like mother made them-no additive. Wet means the scallop is soaked in a phosphate solution, considered safe by the FDA, to retain moisture. If the solution is used, scallops must be labeled.

Prep Time	Cook Time	Yields
5-10 minutes	4-6 minutes	4 servings

1 lb.   sea scallops

Peanut Sauce
¼ C.	peanut butter, smooth or chunky
3 T.	soy sauce
3 T.	rice vinegar
1 tsp.	sugar
½ tsp.	cayenne pepper
2	garlic cloves, minced
2	green onions, chopped

1. Mix peanut sauce ingredients in a medium bowl.
2. Pat scallops very dry.
3. Preheat grill to high.
4. Grill for 2-3 minutes per side.
5. Serve peanut sauce on the side for dipping.

Substitutions: halibut chunks, swordfish, grouper chunks

Tip: *Make scallop kebabs! Set wooden skewers in water to soak for 30 minutes. Skewer scallops, leaving ¼ inch between them. Grill for 2-3 minutes per side.*

Nutrients Per Serving:

Calories	218
Omega-3s	239mg
Total Fat	9g
Saturated Fat	2g
Protein	24g
Total Carbohydrate	9g
Cholesterol	37mg
Sodium	1,036mg
Fiber	1g

Shrimp, Scallop, Vegetable Skewers with Herb Marinade

Prep Time	Cook Time	Yields
15-20 minutes	5-10 minutes	4 servings

12	jumbo raw shrimp, peeled, deveined
12	large sea scallops, trimmed if needed
1	zucchini, in ½-inch slices
1	summer squash, in ½-inch slices
1	red bell pepper, cut into 1-inch squares

Herb Marinade

¼ C.	white wine
2	garlic cloves, minced
2 T.	fresh basil, minced
2 T.	fresh Italian parsley, minced
1 T.	mint, minced
2 T.	olive oil
1 T.	fresh lemon juice
½ tsp.	crushed red pepper flakes
¼ tsp.	salt

1. Soak 12 wooden skewers for 30 minutes in water.
2. Whisk marinade ingredients in bowl. Add shrimp, scallops, zucchini, squash, pepper and toss to coat. Marinate for 30 minutes.
3. Preheat grill to medium-high.
4. On 4 skewers, alternate shrimp and scallops.
5. Thread vegetables on remaining 8 skewers.
6. Cook on greased grill for 2 minutes per side for seafood and 5 minutes per side for vegetables.
7. Serve 1 seafood skewer and 2 vegetable skewers on each plate.

Nutrients Per Serving:

Calories	278
Omega-3s	760mg
Total Fat	10g
Saturated Fat	1g
Protein	35g
Total Carbohydrate	10g
Cholesterol	166g
Sodium	427mg
Fiber	2g

Grilled Squid

Squid cooks quickly-about 45 seconds to 1 minute. Have other meal preparation done before cooking squid.

Prep Time	Cook Time	Yields
5-10 minutes	under 5 minutes	8 servings

2 lbs.   squid steak meat, cut into strips
2 T.   oil

Marinade
¼ C.   dry white wine or broth
¼ C.   fresh lemon juice
6   bay leaves, dried, crushed
2   shallots, minced
2 T.   lemon zest
3 T.   olive oil
½ tsp.   salt
¼ tsp.   pepper

1. Mix marinade ingredients in a self-sealing plastic bag. Put squid into bag. Seal. Refrigerate for 30 minutes.
2. Remove squid from marinade. Pat dry.
3. Preheat grill. Quickly grill squid for 30 seconds per side on oiled grill rack.
4. Boil remaining marinade for 5 minutes and serve along side squid.

Substitutions: squid tubes, tilapia, shrimp

Tip: *Bring seafood up to room temperature before grilling, pan frying or sautéing. This will result in a browner, grill marked coat.*

Nutrients Per Serving:

Calories	171
Omega-3s	301mg
Total Fat	7g
Saturated Fat	1g
Protein	18g
Total Carbohydrate	5g
Cholesterol	264mg
Sodium	196mg
Fiber	1g

Swordfish with Parsley Sauce

Prep Time	Cook Time	Yields
5-10 minutes	8-10 minutes	6 servings

1½ lbs. swordfish steaks
1 T.   olive oil
Salt and pepper, to taste

Fresh Parsley Sauce
½ C.   fresh parsley, minced
2 T.   lemon zest, finely grated
2 T.   olive oil
2 T.   fresh lemon juice
1½ T.   tarragon vinegar
1 T.   fresh chives, minced
1 T.   fresh dill, minced
1 tsp.   sugar
½ tsp.   salt
¼ tsp.   ground pepper

1. Combine all sauce ingredients. Mix well. Cover sauce and refrigerate for at least 1 hour to allow flavors to blend.
2. Preheat grill to high.
3. Brush fish with olive oil, then sprinkle with salt and pepper.
4. Grill on greased grill rack for 4-5 minutes per side, or internal temperature reaches 145°F. at thickest part.
5. Serve parsley sauce alongside.

Substitutions: marlin, tuna, salmon

Nutrients Per Serving:

Calories	202
Omega-3s	963mg
Total Fat	12g
Saturated Fat	2g
Protein	23g
Total Carbohydrate	1g
Cholesterol	44mg
Sodium	395mg
Fiber	1g

Tequila Sea Bass with Chilies

I first tasted this in the Yucatan Peninsula of Mexico. The oranges there are very sweet and delicious. Try using Valencia oranges, which are readily available.

Prep Time	Cook Time	Yields
35 minutes	10 minutes	4 servings

1½ lb. sea bass fillets
Vegetable oil cooking spray

Marinade
⅓ C.   fresh orange juice (about 1 orange)
2   jalapeño chilies, seeded, minced
1   garlic clove, minced
3 T.   fresh lime juice
2 T.   olive oil
1 T.   white tequila
1 tsp.   lime zest
1 tsp.   brown sugar
½ tsp.   paprika
¼ tsp.   salt
Pinch   allspice

1. Whisk all marinade ingredients in a small bowl.
2. Marinate fish in a self sealing plastic bag. Refrigerate for 30 minutes, turning often.
3. Preheat grill to medium-high. Coat fish with oil and grill for 4 minutes, turn and grill until internal temperature of fish reaches 145° F.

Substitutions: swordfish, marlin, tuna

Tip: *Regional varieties of oranges, chilies, garlic and limes make a huge taste difference. You might find them at Farmers Markets across the country as the demand grows for more flavors.*

Nutrients Per Serving:

Calories	248
Omega-3s	610mg
Total Fat	10g
Saturated Fat	2g
Protein	32g
Total Carbohydrate	5g
Cholesterol	70mg
Sodium	117mg
Fiber	1g

Thai-Style Halibut

Prep Time	Cook Time	Yields
5-10 minutes	8-10 minutes	4 servings

1½ lb.	halibut fillet
1 T.	vegetable oil
1 T.	green curry paste
1 T.	fresh ginger root, grated
1 T.	rice wine vinegar
1 tsp.	Thai fish sauce (nam pla)
1 tsp.	sesame oil
2 T.	Thai cilantro, chopped

1. Mix oil, curry paste, ginger, vinegar, fish sauce, sesame oil in a small bowl.
2. Brush sauce onto halibut pieces, coating thoroughly.
3. Cover and refrigerate for 30 minutes.
4. Preheat grill to medium-high.
5. Grill 4 minutes. Turn. Grill until internal temperature reaches 145°F. at thickest part.
6. Garnish with cilantro.

Substitutions: salmon, snapper, tilefish

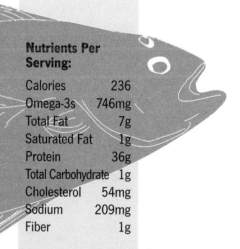

Nutrients Per Serving:

Calories	236
Omega-3s	746mg
Total Fat	7g
Saturated Fat	1g
Protein	36g
Total Carbohydrate	1g
Cholesterol	54mg
Sodium	209mg
Fiber	1g

Grilled Oysters or Clams in the shell

Prep Time	Cook Time	Yields
5 minutes	5-10 minutes	4 servings

**12 large, 20 medium or 32 small oysters or clams
    in the shell**
Jalapeño butter (page 223)

1. Scrub shells thoroughly with a scrub brush. Preheat grill.
2. Crumple a sheet of heavy-duty aluminum foil, place on grill and nestle oysters or clams, lid side up in indentations of foil. (Indentations will keep shellfish from tipping and spilling their liquid.)
3. Grill for 5 to 15 minutes or until shells begin to open. (The larger the shellfish, the longer the cooking time.)
4. Use long-handled tongs to remove shellfish from grill. Use fireproof oven mitts to remove lid of shells. Place oyster knife under the lid of each oyster or clam and pry off the top shell.
5. Top with jalapeño butter, salsa or spritz with lemon or lime juice.

Nutrients Per Serving:

Calories	90
Omega-3s	234mg
Total Fat	3g
Saturated Fat	0g
Protein	16g
Total Carbohydrate	6g
Cholesterol	80g
Sodium	90g
Fiber	0g

Chapter 13

Sauces
Rubs
Butters
Marinades
Salsas
Relishes

Addie's Tartar Sauce

At our wedding, we served a seafood banquet of barbecued salmon and Alaska shrimp with this tartar sauce. The sauce is still requested by relatives and friends. Addie is a wonderful mother-in-law and friend.

Prep Time	Cook Time	Yields
5-10 minutes	None	1 C.

1 C.   low-fat Miracle Whip
2 T.   dill pickle, finely chopped
1 T.   sweet onion, grated
1 T.   fresh lemon juice
¼ tsp.   celery salt

1. Mix all ingredients in a bowl.
2. Cover and refrigerate at least 30 minutes to allow flavors to blend.
3. Serve alongside cooked salmon, shrimp, or other seafood.

Variation: add regular or ½ tsp. Dijon mustard

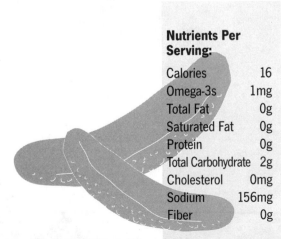

Nutrients Per Serving:

Calories	16
Omega-3s	1mg
Total Fat	0g
Saturated Fat	0g
Protein	0g
Total Carbohydrate	2g
Cholesterol	0mg
Sodium	156mg
Fiber	0g

Red Cocktail Sauce

Prep Time	Cook Time	Yields
5 minutes	None	1 C.

1   8 oz. can tomato sauce
1 tsp.   sugar
¼ tsp.   each: dried thyme, basil, oregano
¼ tsp.   garlic powder
dash   hot sauce

1. Mix all ingredients with a fork until well-combined.
2. Serve with microwaved cod, Poor Man's Lobster, pan-fried catfish or oysters, grlled shrimp.

Variation: add 1 tsp. horseradish sauce. Use ketchup instead of tomato sauce

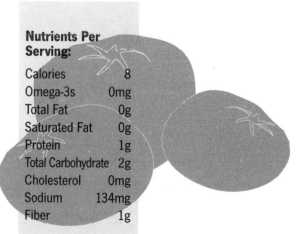

Nutrients Per Serving:

Calories	8
Omega-3s	0mg
Total Fat	0g
Saturated Fat	0g
Protein	1g
Total Carbohydrate	2g
Cholesterol	0mg
Sodium	134mg
Fiber	1g

Seafood Boil Spice Mixture

There are many uses for this spice mixture: rub it on fillets for grilling or broiling, add it to poaching water, or make a soup base for a delicious chowder.

Prep Time	Cook Time	Yields
5 minutes	None	½ C.

1 T.	crushed red pepper flakes
2 tsp.	lemon-pepper
2 tsp.	dried onion flakes
1 tsp.	dried thyme
½ tsp.	garlic powder
1	bay leaf
¼ C.	salt

1. Combine all ingredients.
2. Store in a dark, cool place in an airtight container or bag.

To use:
1. Dissolve spice mixture in one gallon boiling water.
2. Boil 2-3 pounds of seafood, such as shrimp, crab, or crawfish, vegetables, such as potatoes and corn, until done.
3. Drain and serve hot.

Tip: *Strain, refrigerate and save broth for another day's meal. If keeping it longer than three days, freeze broth.*

Nutrients Per Mixture:

Calories	80
Omega-3s	0mg
Total Fat	0g
Saturated Fat	0g
Protein	0g
Total Carbohydrate	0g
Cholesterol	0mg
Sodium	224mg
Fiber	0g

Jamaican Spice Rub

Prep Time	Cook Time	Yields
5 minutes	None	2/3 C.

¼ C.   granulated white sugar
2 T.   celery salt
1 T.   dark brown sugar
1 T.   onion flakes
1½ tsp. garlic salt
1 tsp.   chili powder
1 tsp.   black pepper
¼ tsp.   allspice
¼ tsp.   cayenne pepper
¼ tsp.   ground cloves

Tip: Add 1 *teaspoon curry powder to make an East Indian flavor. It's an excellent seasoning to add to rice.*

1. Mix all ingredients in an airtight container.
2. To use, coat seafood with a little olive oil.
3. Rub in about 2 teaspoons of seasoning onto chosen seafood. Bake, broil, or grill as desired.

Nutrients Per Serving:

Calories   25
Omega-3s   4mg
Total Fat   0g
Saturated Fat   0g
Protein   0g
Total Carbohydrate 6g
Cholesterol   0mg
Sodium   723mg
Fiber   1g

Classic Salmon Spice Rub

This rub is our family favorite, used on boatloads of seafood caught by my father. Dad's Wild King salmon was served at our wedding.

Prep Time	Cook Time	Yields
5 minutes	None	12 servings (¾ C.)

½ C. plus 2 T. brown sugar
1 T.   whole, dry oregano
1 ½ tsp. whole, dry thyme
1 ½ tsp. chili powder
¾ tsp.   garlic powder
¾ tsp.   onion powder
¼ tsp.   cayenne pepper

1. Mix all ingredients well.
2. Store in an airtight bag or container.
3. To use: cover salmon with 1 tablespoon olive oil.
4. Lightly sprinkle salmon with salt.
5. Evenly rub on 1 tablespoon Classic Salmon Spice Rub on both sides of skinless fish.
6. Bake, broil, or grill as desired.

Tips: *Rub spices on fish or shrimp and set on counter for 20 minutes to "cure". The air movement in the kitchen will dry the fish which will result in beautiful grill marks on top of the fish. Evenly sprinkle mixture on seafood.*

Add ¼ tsp Hickory smoke salt for a tasty new flavor.

Nutrients Per Serving:

Calories	21
Omega-3s	20mg
Total Fat	0mg
Saturated Fat	0mg
Protein	0mg
Total Carbohydrate	5g
Cholesterol	0mg
Sodium	5mg
Fiber	1g

Homemade Old Bay

This doesn't taste exactly like Old Bay seasoning – we think it tastes much better. Look in your grocery store Mexican food section for bulk spices – they are much less expensive.

Prep Time	Cook Time	Yields
5-10 minutes	None	½ C.

12	bay leaves, crushed
2 T.	celery seeds
2 T.	black pepper
2 tsp.	sweet paprika
1 tsp.	ground cardamon
1 tsp.	mustard seed
½ tsp.	mace (optional)
8	whole cloves

Tip: Buy a coffee mill that will be a dedicated spice grinder. Fresh ground spices are full of more flavor than the pre-ground ones you purchase at the store. Grind just what you'll need at one time.

1. Clean a coffee grinder by using a damp paper towel.
2. Mix all spices and grind until completely fine.
3. Store in an airtight container until ready to use.
4. To use, rub or sprinkle before baking, broiling or grilling fish. Also great for shellfish!

Substitutions: To substitute ground cardamon, buy the pods, open and grind the tiny black seeds inside until you have the proper amount.

Nutrients Per Serving:

Calories	5
Omega-3s	10mg
Total Fat	0mg
Saturated Fat	0mg
Protein	0g
Total Carbohydrate	1g
Cholesterol	0mg
Sodium	1mg
Fiber	1g

Basil Butter

Prep Time	**Cook Time**	**Yields**
5 minutes	less than a minute	24 tsp. (½ C.)

¼ C.   butter
¼ C.   olive oil
1 T.   dried basil
1 tsp.   white pepper
1 tsp.   lemon-pepper seasoning

1. Soften butter for 5 seconds in microwave.
2. Mix butter and olive oil together in a bowl.
3. Add all other ingredients and blend well with a spoon.
4. Freeze for 30 minutes to firm up if it is too soft.
5. Place one teaspoon over a serving of freshly grilled or broiled seafood.

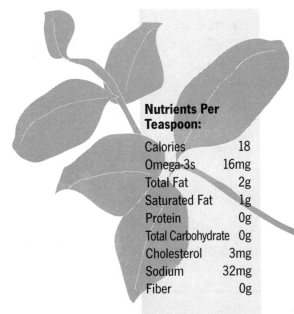

Nutrients Per Teaspoon:

Calories	18
Omega-3s	16mg
Total Fat	2g
Saturated Fat	1g
Protein	0g
Total Carbohydrate	0g
Cholesterol	3mg
Sodium	32mg
Fiber	0g

Ginger-Garlic Butter

Prep Time	Cook Time	Yields
5 minutes	less than a minute	12 tsp. (¼ C.)

2 T.	butter
2 T.	olive oil
1	garlic clove, finely minced
2 tsp.	fresh ginger root, grated
2 tsp.	fresh lemon juice
Dash	white pepper

1. Soften butter for 5 seconds in microwave.
2. Mix butter and olive oil together in a bowl.
3. Add all other ingredients and blend well with a spoon.
4. Freeze for 30 minutes to firm up if it is too soft.
5. Serve over freshly grilled or broiled seafood.

Substitutions: Soy sauce instead of lemon juice for a new flavor

Tip: *At the grocery store, you can break off just the amount you need; you don't have to take a whole big ginger root.*

Nutrients Per Teaspoon:

Calories	18
Omega-3s	0mg
Total Fat	2g
Saturated Fat	1g
Protein	0g
Total Carbohydrate	0g
Cholesterol	7mg
Sodium	18mg
Fiber	0g

Herb Butter

Prep Time	Cook Time	Yields
5 minutes	less than a minute	24 tsp. (½ C.)

¼ C.	butter
¼ C.	olive oil
2	garlic cloves, minced
1 T.	fresh parsley, minced
1 T.	fresh lemon juice
1 T.	fresh herbs, such as basil, oregano, rosemary, or thyme (or 1 tsp. dried herbs)

1. Soften butter for 5 seconds in microwave.
2. Mix butter and olive oil in a bowl.
3. Add all other ingredients and blend well with a spoon.
4. Freeze for 30 minutes to firm up if it is too soft.
5. Serve over freshly grilled or broiled seafood. Use as a dipping sauce for steamed clams or mussels.

Substitutions: For a richer spread, use all butter and omit olive oil

Tip: *Roll in the shape of a log, cover with plastic wrap and freeze. Slice off frozen sections as needed.*

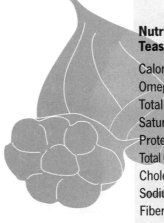

Nutrients Per Teaspoon:

Calories	18
Omega-3s	13mg
Total Fat	2g
Saturated Fat	1g
Protein	0g
Total Carbohydrate	0g
Cholesterol	3mg
Sodium	18mg
Fiber	0g

Jalapeño Butter

Prep Time	Cook Time	Yields
5 minutes	less than a minute	24 tsp.

¼ C.	butter
¼ C.	olive oil
¼ C.	fresh cilantro, minced
2	jalapeño peppers, seeded, chopped
2	garlic cloves, minced
dash	hot sauce

1. Soften butter for 5 seconds in microwave.
2. Mix butter and olive oil together in a bowl.
3. Add all other ingredients and blend well with a spoon.
4. Freeze for 30 minutes to firm up if it is too soft.
5. Serve over freshly grilled, broiled, or poached seafood.

Tip: *Freeze remaining butter in ice cube trays and place in a freezer bag for easy use later on.*

Nutrients Per Teaspoon:

Calories	18
Omega-3s	13mg
Total Fat	2g
Saturated Fat	1g
Protein	0g
Total Carbohydrate	0g
Cholesterol	7mg
Sodium	19mg
Fiber	0g

Pesto Butter

Prep Time	Cook Time	Yields
5 minutes	less than a minute	24 tsp.

2 T.	butter
2 T.	olive oil
½ C.	fresh basil, loosely packed, minced
¼ C.	Parmesan cheese, grated
2 T.	fresh parsley
1 T.	fresh lemon juice
¼ tsp.	black pepper

1. Soften butter for 5 seconds in microwave.
2. Mix butter and olive oil together in a bowl.
3. Add all other ingredients and blend well with a spoon.
4. Freeze for 30 minutes to firm up if it is too soft.
5. Place 1 teaspoon over a serving of freshly grilled or broiled seafood.

Substitutions: Add 2 T. pine nuts finely chopped, omit butter

Tip: *To soften butter, remove it from refrigerator an hour before use.*

Nutrients Per Teaspoon:

Calories	21
Omega-3s	15mg
Total Fat	2g
Saturated Fat	1g
Protein	0g
Total Carbohydrate	0g
Cholesterol	3mg
Sodium	31mg
Fiber	0g

Sun-Dried Tomato Butter

This topping is one of our family favorites spread on halibut roasted on a wood baking plank.

Prep Time	Cook Time	Yields
5 minutes	less than a minute	½ C.

2 T.	butter
2 T.	olive oil
¼ C.	sun-dried tomatoes, chopped
1 T.	fresh parsley, minced
1 T.	scallions, minced
1 T.	orange peel, grated

Tip: *Can easily be doubled or tripled for more servings.*

1. Soften butter for 5 seconds in microwave.
2. Mix butter and olive oil together in a bowl.
3. Add all other ingredients and blend well with a spoon.
4. Freeze for 30 minutes to firm up if it is too soft.
5. Serve over freshly grilled or broiled seafood.

Substitutions: For a richer butter, use all butter and omit olive oil

Nutrients Per Teaspoon:

Calories	19
Omega-3s	14mg
Total Fat	2g
Saturated Fat	1g
Protein	0g
Total Carbohydrate	0g
Cholesterol	3mg
Sodium	41mg
Fiber	0g

Basil or Almond Pesto

Prep Time	Cook Time	Yields
10-15 minutes	None	16 servings (2 C.)

2½ C.	fresh basil
¼ C.	pine nuts
¼ C.	Parmesan cheese, grated
2 T.	fresh parsley, chopped
4	garlic cloves, minced
½ tsp.	salt
½ C.	olive oil

1. Blend all ingredients except olive oil in a food processor until finely chopped.
2. Add oil in a fine stream, with machine still running, continue to blend until mixture forms a smooth green paste. If it isn't smooth, add a little more oil until it is. Be careful not to add too much oil.
3. Serve immediately over baked seafood. Toast a sliced whole grain baguette to serve alongside.

Almond Pesto:
Substitute 2½ cups fresh, chopped Italian parsley for basil.
Substitute an equal amount of chopped raw almonds for pine nuts.

Tip: *Make pesto while your basil is thriving, freeze pesto in small packages for the rest of the year. Don't use dried spices; the flavor won't be the same. If you store the pesto in a jar in the refrigerator, put a thin layer of olive oil on top of the pesto to prevent the basil from turning brown. Just stir in the olive oil before using.*

Nutrients Per Serving:

Calories	63
Omega-3s	63mg
Total Fat	6g
Saturated Fat	1g
Protein	1g
Total Carbohydrate	1g
Cholesterol	1mg
Sodium	93mg
Fiber	1g

Minted Turkish Marinade

Prep Time	Cook Time	Yields
5 minutes	None	10 servings (1¼ C.)

1 C.   plain, low fat yogurt
½ C.   fresh mint leaves, minced
3   garlic cloves, minced
2 T.   fresh lemon juice
1 T.   grated lemon zest
1 tsp. salt
½ tsp. ground allspice
½ tsp. ground cinnamon
¼ tsp. cayenne pepper

Tip: *Also can be used as a dipping sauce for kebabs! Wonderful as a topping for fish tacos.*

1. Combine all ingredients in a small bowl and whisk until smooth.
2. Use to marinate fish such as halibut, tilapia, blue fish or pollock.

Nutrients Per Serving:

Calories	19
Omega-3s	9mg
Total Fat	1g
Saturated Fat	1g
Protein	1g
Total Carbohydrate	2g
Cholesterol	10mg
Sodium	250mg
Fiber	1g

Spicy Barbeque Marinade

Prep Time	Cook Time	Yields
5 minutes	None	8 servings (1 C.)

¼ C.   onion, thinly sliced
¼ C.   fresh lime juice
1 T.   reduced-sodium soy sauce
1 T.   brown sugar
2 tsp.   ground coriander
1 tsp.   ground cumin
1 tsp.   salt
1 tsp.   pepper
1 tsp.   crushed red pepper flakes
½ tsp.   ground ginger
2 T.   olive oil

1. Combine all ingredients except oil in a small bowl.
2. Slowly whisk in a little oil at a time until mixture is blended.
3. Marinade may be stored, covered, in refrigerator for up to one week.

Nutrients Per Serving:

Calories	51
Omega-3s	29mg
Total Fat	4g
Saturated Fat	1g
Protein	1g
Total Carbohydrate	4g
Cholesterol	0mg
Sodium	593mg
Fiber	1g

Sassy Salsa

I keep a big jar of store-bought salsa on hand and use it as a base to make homemade salsa.

Prep Time	Cook Time	Yields
5-10 minutes	None	2 C.

1½ C.	mild salsa from the store
½	small onion, finely diced
1	tomato, diced
½ C.	fresh cilantro, minced
1	small lime, juiced
1	Jalapeño or Anaheim pepper, seeded and finely diced

1. Mix all ingredients.
2. Cover and refrigerate for at least 10 minutes to blend flavors.
3. Top on freshly grilled oysters in the shell. Mix with cooked shrimp and serve in a cocktail glass decorated with shredded lettuce. Fill a ripe, halved, pitted avocado with salsa and top with cooked crab or shrimp meat. Garnish with chopped parsley or cilantro.

Substitutions: Fresh parsley in place of cilantro; select peppers according to your "heat" level; combine any color of chopped bell pepper to add color and crunch.

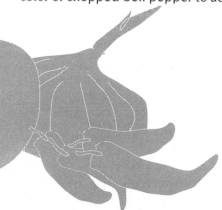

Nutrients Per Serving:

Calories	17
Omega-3s	2mg
Total Fat	0mg
Saturated Fat	0mg
Protein	1g
Total Carbohydrate	4g
Cholesterol	0mg
Sodium	73mg
Fiber	8g

Pear-Pepper Salsa

Prep Time	Cook Time	Yields
5-10 minutes	None	1 ½ C.

2	pears, diced
¼ C.	raisins
¼ C.	red bell pepper, seeded and diced
2	green onions, sliced thinly
1	jalapeño pepper, seeded and diced
1 T.	rice vinegar
½ tsp.	curry powder

1. Mix all ingredients.
2. Cover and refrigerate for at least 10 minutes to allow flavors to blend.
3. Serve on freshly baked, grilled, poached or broiled seafood.

Substitutions: Dried cranberries instead of raisins

Tip: *Salsas are a calorie-saver when served instead of fat laden tarter sauces.*

Nutrients Per Serving:

Calories	54
Omega-3s	5mg
Total Fat	0g
Saturated Fat	0g
Protein	1g
Total Carbohydrate	14g
Cholesterol	0mg
Sodium	2mg
Fiber	2g

Cranberry Salsa

Prep Time	Cook Time	Yields
5-10 minutes	10 minutes	4 servings

1   8-oz. can whole cranberry sauce
¼ C.   picante sauce
¼ C.   orange juice
1 tsp.   orange zest
½ tsp. dried oregano

Tip: Use fresh cranberries when in season.

1. Mix all ingredients in a saucepan.
2. Bring to a boil.
3. Reduce heat and simmer for 10 minutes.
4. Serve hot with your favorite cooked fish.

Substitutions: Lemon or lime juice and zest for the orange juice and zest.

Nutrients Per Serving:

Calories	94
Omega-3	5mg
Total Fat	0g
Saturated Fat	0g
Protein	1g
Total Carbohydrate	9g
Cholesterol	0mg
Sodium	0mg
Fiber	2g

Mango Salsa

*Many a gray foggy Seattle day has been wiped away when
we turn up the Hawaiian music and broil seafood. Mango
salsa topped mahi-mahi helps us hula back to Hawaii in our
dreams.*

Prep Time	Cook Time	Yields
5-10 minutes	None	1½ C.

2	ripe mangos, peeled, diced
⅓ C.	red onion, finely diced
⅓ C.	fresh cilantro, diced
1	red Serrano or jalapeño pepper, seeded, minced
1	fresh lime, juiced
1 tsp.	ginger powder
½ tsp.	salt

1. Mix all ingredients in a medium bowl.
2. Taste and adjust seasonings.
3. Cover and refrigerate for at least 10 minutes to allow flavors to blend.
4. Serve on freshly grilled or broiled seafood.

Substitutions: Fresh parsley in place of cilantro

Tip: *If you want more heat in your salsa don't remove the seeds from the chili peppers. You may want to wear gloves while working with hot chili peppers. Wash hands afterwards, being careful to not touch your face or eyes.*

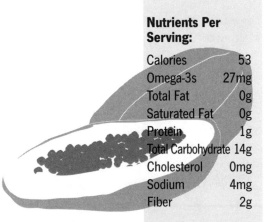

Nutrients Per Serving:

Calories	53
Omega-3s	27mg
Total Fat	0g
Saturated Fat	0g
Protein	1g
Total Carbohydrate	14g
Cholesterol	0mg
Sodium	4mg
Fiber	2g

Pineapple Chutney

Prep Time	Cook Time	Yields
5-10 minutes	5 minutes	2 C.

1	8 oz. can crushed pineapple
½ C.	apple, chopped
½ C.	red bell pepper, seeded and chopped
¼ C.	sweet onion, chopped
3 T.	sugar
2 T.	balsamic vinegar
1 tsp.	ground mustard seed
¼ tsp.	salt

1. Mix all ingredients in a small saucepan.
2. Simmer for 5 minutes, stirring constantly.
3. Serve hot or cold.

Substitutions: Canned mandarin oranges for pineapple

Nutrients Per Serving:

Calories	48
Omega-3s	21mg
Total Fat	0g
Saturated Fat	0g
Protein	1g
Total Carbohydrate	12g
Cholesterol	0mg
Sodium	74mg
Fiber	1g

Blueberry Relish

Native berries and local caught seafood have gone together for centuries. Norwegians use lingonberries, Northwest Natives savor raspberries and salmon berries, Maine has bushels of blueberries and huckleberries.

Prep Time	**Cook Time**	**Yields**
5 minutes	5 minutes	8 servings (2 C.)

2 C.	blueberries
¾ C.	sugar
½ C.	water
½ tsp.	ground allspice
½ tsp.	cinnamon
¼ tsp.	ground cloves

Tip: *Add chopped cilantro and onion for an all new taste.*

1. Combine all ingredients in a saucepan.
2. Bring slowly to a boil, reduce heat to low, simmer for 5 minutes, stirring occasionally.
3. Serve hot or cold under or over fish such as salmon, trout, tilapia, cod, grouper. Berry relish is especially savory with pan seared sea scallops.

Substitutions: Brown sugar or honey instead of white sugar

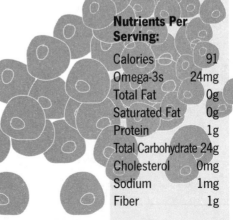

Nutrients Per Serving:

Calories	91
Omega-3s	24mg
Total Fat	0g
Saturated Fat	0g
Protein	1g
Total Carbohydrate	24g
Cholesterol	0mg
Sodium	1mg
Fiber	1g

Corn Relish

There are over 35 different varieties of garlic. Rojo (red) garlic adds a zip and makes the relish much more colorful.

Prep Time	Cook Time	Yields
5-10 minutes	None	4 servings

3	Rojo garlic cloves, minced
2 C.	frozen sweet corn
1	red bell pepper, seeded, chopped
1	green bell pepper, seeded, chopped
1	4 oz. can green chilies, chopped
1 T.	lime juice
1 tsp.	ground cumin

1. Mix all ingredients in a large bowl.
2. Cover, refrigerate until corn is thawed.
3. Serve chilled with your favorite cooked fish, or with tortilla chips.

Substitutions: Add a small can of drained black beans, chopped tomatillos, cilantro; adjust the seasonings to taste.

Nutrients Per Serving:

Calories	23
Omega-3	1 mg
Total Fat	0g
Saturated Fat	0g
Protein	0g
Total Carbohydrate	18mg
Cholesterol	0mg
Sodium	60mg
Fiber	10

Bibliography

Hansen, E. *Seafood Grilling Twice a Week*. **Richmond Beach**, **Wash.: National Seafood Educators, 2001.**

Mahan, L. Kathleen, Escott-Stump, Sylvia, *Krause's Food, Nutrition & Diet Therapy*, 11th **Edition, W.B. Saunders Company 2006**

McGee, Howard, *On Food and Cooking, The Science and Lore of the Kitchen*, **Scribner, 2004**

Nesheim, Malden C., and **Yaktine, Ann L**., editors, *Committee on Nutrient Relationships in Seafood*, *Seafood Choices*, National Institute of Health, 2006

Pigott, George M., Barbee W. Tucker, *Seafood; Effects of Technology on Nutrition* **Marcel Dekker, Inc, 1990**

Simopoulos, A. P., Jo Robinson. *The Omega Plan: The Medically Proven Diet That Restores Your Body's Essential Nutritional Balance.* **New York: HarperCollins, 1998.**

Stoll, A. L. *The Omega-3 Connection: The Groundbreaking Omega-3 Antidepression Diet and Brain Program.* **New York: Simon & Schuster, 2001.**

NUTRITION SITES TO SET YOUR SIGHTS ON

Consider adding these credible expert Web sites to your list of "favorites" to help you differentiate fact from fiction. Check them regularly.

www.aafp.org   www.iflc.org
www.americanheart.org   www.medicineplus.gov
www.berkelywellness.com   www.mayoclinic.org
www.eatright.org   www.noaa.org
www.healthfinder.org   www.nhlbi.nih.gov

Subject Index

Subject Index

Subject Index

Subject Index

Ordering Information

Please send me copies of

Seafood Omega-3s For Healthy Living	___ @ $16.95 ea.	_____
Seafood Grilling Twice a Week	___ @ $14.95 ea.	_____
Seafood Twice a Week	___ @ $14.95 ea.	_____
	Subtotal	_____
Washington residents add sales tax	(subtotal x 8.8%)	_____
Shipping and Handling	$3.50	_____
	TOTAL	_____

Method of Payment: ☐ Check   ☐ Money Order
                    ☐ Visa   ☐ Mastercard
                    ☐ Discover   ☐ American Express

Name of Cardholder _____

Account #_____ Expires_____

Signature _____

Bill to:

Name _____

Address _____

City _____ State_____ Zip_____

Phone _____ Fax_____

Email _____

Ship to:

Name _____

Address _____

City _____ State_____ Zip_____

Mail payment to: **National Seafood Educators**
                     P.O. Box 60006
                     Richmond Beach, WA 98160

www.seafoodeducators.com
Phone: 206-546-6410   Fax: 206-546-6411

Please list bookstores, gift shops, or seafood markets in your area that would be interested in handling this book.

Name _____ Phone_____

Name _____ Phone_____